Capturing Change

Globalizing the Curriculum through Technology

Anne Sauder Wall
Carlette Jackson Hardin
Ann Shelby Harris

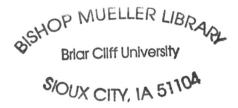
Published in partnership with the
American Forum for Global Education

Rowman & Littlefield Education
Lanham, Maryland • Toronto • Oxford
2005

Published in partnership with the
American Forum for Global Education

Published in the United States of America
by Rowman & Littlefield Education
A Division of Rowman & Littlefield Publishers, Inc., a wholly owned
subsidiary of The Rowman & Littlefield Publishing Group, Inc.
4501 Forbes Boulevard, Suite 200, Lanham, Maryland 20706
www.rowmaneducation.com

PO Box 317
Oxford
OX2 9RU, UK

British Library Cataloguing in Publication Information Available

Library of Congress Cataloging-in-Publication Data

Wall, Anne Sauder.
  Capturing change : globalizing the curriculum through technology / Anne
Sauder Wall, Carlette Jackson Hardin, Ann Shelby Harris.
       p. cm.
  Includes bibliographical references and index.
  ISBN 1-57886-289-2 (hardcover : alk. paper) — ISBN 1-57886-296-5
(pbk. : alk. paper)
    1. Curriculum planning—Technological innovations—United States. 2.
Education and globalization—United States. 3. Educational technology—
United States. 4. Educational change—United States. I. Hardin, Carlette
Jackson. II. Harris, Ann Shelby, 1939– . III. Title.
  LB2806.15.W36 2005   BK
  375'.0028—dc22 $29.95   2005009255

To my husband, Bill, who climbs to the top of mountains and shares the view with me.
—Anne Wall

For my grandson, Drew, with hope that this book might help create classrooms in which he will learn to be accepting and tolerant of all people.
—Carlette Hardin

To my family for their gifts of love, inspiration, and humor that sustain me.
—Ann Harris

Throughout this book you will find numerous references to specific websites, with the URLs appearing at the end of each chapter. All of the websites were working and available at the time this book was written; however, this might change due to the unpredictable nature of the Internet. If a website is no longer available, please check the Capturing Change website at http://capturingchange.com for an updated address or alternative site.

Contents

THEORIES AND STANDARDS

Part 1 of this book provides a review of two recent additions to the K–12 curriculum: global education and technology. The union of global education and technology provides students with the tools necessary to successfully participate in an ever-evolving global world. Chapter 1 introduces the philosophy, history, and criticism of global education, and chapter 2 describes how technology provides opportunities for teachers to advance the concepts of global education by connecting students to the world. Four model strategies approved by the International Society for Technology in Education are identified as a means of integrating technology across all disciplines and advancing a global curriculum.

CHAPTER 1

An Introduction to the Global Curriculum

> I understand that when some of you received your invitations to this dinner you replied, "There must be some mistake; I'm only a teacher." A more apt response would have been, "It's about time; after all, I am a teacher." And the rest of your sentence would have been, "If you want to influence the shape of the 21st century, you better start with me."
>
> —Madeleine K. Albright, former secretary of state, at a dinner honoring international education, Nov. 29, 2000, Washington, DC (http://www.rpcv.org/pages/sitepage.cfm?id=242)

Educators teaching in the twenty-first century face challenges never encountered by the generations of teachers before them. Recognizing that knowledge about the three "Rs" is only the foundation of what students will need to know to have successful lives in the twenty-first century, teachers realize that students now need three new skills—*the ability to learn, the ability to change,* and *the ability to accept*—to be prepared for the century ahead.

Today's students must have skills beyond memorizing necessary facts, and they must know *how to learn* so that they can manage the ever-increasing amount of new information presented to them daily. Students will live in a world of constant change, and successful students will be those who can *adapt to change* and who in turn become agents of change. Finally, realizing that events occurring across the world today will affect students' lives tomorrow, teachers must prepare students to *accept their role* as citizens of a global society rather than simply seeing themselves as citizens of a single state or nation. In fact,

Tye and Tye (1992) suggest that global awareness will become the new basic skill of the twenty-first century.

The need for global awareness is apparent when you consider that students who enter kindergarten today will confront a world quite different from that of their twentieth-century parents and grandparents. Their daily contacts will include individuals from diverse ethnic, linguistic, racial, and socioeconomic backgrounds. Through advances in technology, members of future generations will have daily discussions with people from around the world, buy and sell items with a single keystroke, and view worlds beyond our galaxy.

Unfortunately, they will also experience some of history's most serious health problems, increasing inequities between less developed and more developed nations, environmental deterioration, and overpopulation. They will be challenged to overcome a lack of tolerance for others who are culturally and racially different, an uneven distribution of resources, ethnic conflicts, and struggles for power. Students of the twenty-first century will face tremendous challenges to their emotional, intellectual, and physical well-being.

Hendrix (1998) states that global awareness is especially needed for students in the United States, who tend to be unaware of the contributions and perspectives of other races, nations, and cultures. That is because educators from the United States have emphasized the human experience from North American and European perspectives, often presenting an uncritical, chauvinistic view of the world with the United States and its citizens as superior to the rest of the world. If students are not exposed to other cultures, this sense of superiority can lead to biases and patronizing attitudes toward other people. When students explore such complex issues as human values, global systems, and global problems, however, they will be less likely to develop an inflated sense of self or group superiority. Therefore, the philosophical foundation for global education is the affirmation of our common unity with people throughout the world.

HISTORY OF GLOBAL EDUCATION

The first attention to a global curriculum occurred in the years following World War II, when it became increasingly obvious that the United States (and indeed all nations) had entered into a totally new relationship with each other and with planet earth. With a realization that the technology existed to destroy the earth and its people, there was a need to reexamine what schools were teaching students regarding relationships with others. Then, with the launching of *Sputnik* in 1958, schools pushed for more involvement in social studies and second-language programs. Unfortunately, these movements toward global awareness were based more on fear than on a desire for acceptance and tolerance.

The 1960s brought more attention to the need for a global agenda as citizens faced worldwide issues such as resource shortages, the arms race, immigration, unemployment, and overpopulation. Hendrix (1998) states that a new stimulus to global education came with the opening of the Second World Food Congress in 1963 in Washington, D.C., by President John F. Kennedy. Kennedy's words brought global issues to the forefront of the political agenda and helped start the contemporary global education movement. Other contributing factors in the 1960s and 1970s were the civil rights movement, the Vietnam War, criticism of monocultural textbooks, and discussions among world leaders regarding the possibilities of world economic and social progress. By the end of the late 1970s, this new emphasis on global awareness was known as "global education" or the "global perspective."

During the 1980s and 1990s, global educators taught young people to understand others through dimensions of global education that included issues of local/global connections, perspective consciousness, cross-cultural alikeness, global history, and economic, political, ecological, and technological systems around the globe. Educators often used popular metaphors such as the "global village" or "spaceship earth" and slogans such as "think globally, act locally" to help their students envision their place and choices in a global age. Centers for global education were created across the country to provide materials and workshops for teachers.

Until the mid-1980s, the movement toward global perspectives in education went unchallenged (Schukar, 1993). Several challenges to global education, however, were initiated in the mid-1980s as global education became a controversial issue. Many saw global education as a threat to U.S. supremacy. Because of this perceived threat, the global education movement in the United States adopted a number of ethnocentric characteristics (Tye, 2003). Since the latter part of the 1990s, global educators have tried to avoid issues that were controversial by striving for what is euphemistically called "balance." Although educators were still encouraged to teach about other peoples and countries, they were encouraged to do so "patriotically." In fact, many teachers and schools have abandoned global education programs entirely because of the fear of community reprisal.

World events of the early part of the twenty-first century have brought a renewed examination of how global awareness is taught. It has become apparent that the United States cannot seclude itself from the problems, needs, and concerns of the rest of the world. If students are to become effective U.S. citizens, they must also find their place in the global village. More than ever, students need a global education. Global education has gained new momentum and plays an increasing role in the United States and the world. Global education has come of age, and, as Kirkwood (2001) states, "global education offers teachers opportunities to guide students on their twenty-first century journey to shape a more peaceful world" (p. 15).

DEFINING GLOBAL EDUCATION

There is no universally acceptable definition of global education, and the label is attached to similar educational initiatives around the world, including development education, perspectives in education, intercultural education, and world studies. The search for meaning is a recurrent theme in global education research and writing.

A search for a definition of global education can begin by indicating what global education is not. This is necessary because "global education" can be a misleading phrase. As a term, "global education" appears to be similar to history education, mathematics, science education, and so on. However, global education is very different from content-bound subjects in that these subjects are identified as having particular characteristics or specific content and subject matter. Global education is not defined in terms of a particular body of content, subject matter, or discipline.

Adding to the confusion is the fact that there are other educational models that appear similar in nature to global education. Often confused with global education is the concept of international education.

Although international education has existed longer than global education, its curriculum has usually been limited to studying nations, geographic areas, and cultures. Global education includes similar studies of particular nations but also focuses on social change, global problem solving, global issues, and interacting, interdependent global systems.

Global education is also often compared to multicultural education. Chanda (1992) defines multicultural education as the study of the ideas, customs, skills, and arts of different people at a given period of time. It provides the knowledge, skills, and attitudes needed to live effectively in a pluralistic society. This definition encompasses the issues of racism, gender, and sexual preference. Merryfield (1995) suggests that global and multicultural education overlap in their goals to develop multiple perspectives and multiple loyalties, strengthen cultural consciousness and intercultural competence, respect human dignity and human rights, and combat prejudice and discrimination. Table 1.1 provides a comparison of global education and similar education models that focus on global issues.

Table 1.1   A Comparison of Global Education and Similar Education Models.

Educational Model	Global Education
Multicultural education is education that includes the ideas, customs, skills, arts, and so forth of different people at a given period of time.	Global education has a similar perspective, but includes the concept of the global village with increasing interdependence between nations.
Development education promotes social change through education. It aims to raise awareness and understanding of how global issues affect the everyday lives of individuals.	Global education is perceived to be in the common interest of all people and the planet. Personal growth rather than national development is the goal.
International education focuses on problem solving and conflict resolution within particular countries. Problems and issues inherent to cultures and nations are explored.	Global education includes similar studies of countries but also focuses on social change and promotes global problem solving.
Peace education or world order education represents an old form of international education. The focus of peace education is the promotion of world peace and the reduction of international tensions.	Global and peace education share common concerns over issues such as human rights, self-determination, international conflict management, and conflict resolution.
Ethnocentric education is a form of nationalism designed to win the allegiance of students to a particular culture.	Global education challenges students to see themselves as citizens of the world rather than focusing on an allegiance to a particular state or nation.

Because global education is not content bound, it is difficult to find *the* definition for global education. Part of the problem is that there is no agreement among the advocates of global education about the philosophical basis of the movement. Gilliom (1981) states that, in essence, "global education can be thought of as those educational efforts designed to cultivate in young people a global perspective and to develop in them the knowledge, skills, and attitudes needed to live effectively in a world possessing limited natural resources and characterized by ethnic diversity, cultural pluralism, and increasing interdependence" (p. 170). Kirkwood (2001) suggests that the philosophical underpinnings of global education rest on the following assumptions: 1) human beings are created equal regardless of age, ability, class, ethnicity, gender, nationality, sexual orientation, socioeconomic status, or race; 2) human behavior is culturally, not racially, determined; 3) all members of the human family possess basic human rights; and 4) global education has a moral purpose.

In 1975, Robert Hanvey provided one of the most accepted definitions of global education by suggesting that global education consists of five interdisciplinary dimensions:

1. *Perspective consciousness* provides students with an understanding of the multiple perspectives held by people and nations around the world. Through perspective consciousness, students develop recognition that others have views of the world that are profoundly different from their own.
2. *State-of-the-planet awareness* helps students develop an in-depth understanding of the prevailing global issues, events, and conditions. It provides an understanding of the causes of events and their effects on nations and people.
3. *Cross-cultural awareness* provides a general understanding of the defining characteristics of world cultures with an emphasis on understanding similarities and differences. It emphasizes the diversity of ideas and practices in human societies and how the ideas and ways of one's own culture are perceived from others' points of view.
4. *Knowledge of global dynamics* provides a familiarity with the nature of systems and an introduction to complex international systems. It provides an understanding of how all people are linked in patterns of interdependence and dependence in a variety of ways.

5. *Awareness of human choices* challenges students to understand the problems of choice confronting individuals and nations. It provides a review of strategies for action on issues in local, national, and international settings.

Tye and Tye (1990, 1992) provide a definition of global education that integrates or combines many elements of Hanvey's original definition. They suggest that global education involves the following:

- The study of problems and issues that cut across national boundaries and the interconnectedness of the economic, environmental, cultural, political, and technological systems involved.
- The skill of perspective taking that requires being able to see life from someone else's point of view. The goal is the realization that although individuals and groups may view life differently, they also have common needs and wants.

Merryfield (1997) combined the five elements advanced by Hanvey into an all-inclusive definition of global education, creating what many consider to be the most up-to-date framework in the field today. She included eight elements: human beliefs and values, global systems, global issues and problems, cross-cultural understanding, awareness of human choices, global history, acquisition of indigenous knowledge, and development of analytical, evaluative, and participatory skills.

THE GLOBAL EDUCATION CONTROVERSY

After a review of the philosophies that are the essence of global education, it is hard to imagine that educators, politicians, and parents have not embraced them. Yet the teaching of a global curriculum remains a controversial topic. Since the 1970s, there have been criticisms and attacks on a global curriculum from many fronts.

Some attacks come from politicians and policymakers who argue that global education represents the views of the political left. They are concerned that the redistribution of world resources and wealth is overemphasized in the curriculum and that teaching materials discourage the concept of national sovereignty. Politicians and policymakers with an anti–global education agenda stress that cooperation is overemphasized and that competition is downplayed. They view global education at odds with patriotism and national loyalty.

According to Tye (2003), much of this concern comes from the fact that schooling is still seen as a major force in the building of national loyalties. Opponents have suggested that the term "global" is antithetical to one of the fundamental purposes of education, which is to build loyalty toward U.S. political, economic, and sociocultural institutions and ideas. Politicians and educators alike, therefore, fear that global or international education is contradictory to the fundamental purpose of school—to prepare young people to be citizens of the United States.

At the same time that students are taught to become citizens of particular nations, however, they also need to understand that the world in which they live extends beyond national identities. Perhaps this is truer now than in any other period of history, as the students of the twenty-first century will face issues that are international and global in scope. Such issues as environmental pollution, epidemic disease, poverty, and the threat of nuclear war affect people everywhere regardless of their geographic location and national identification.

Some U.S. citizens fear that global awareness requires the abdication of national values. Ramler (1991) stresses, however, that there is never a need for a contradiction between global understanding and national values and interests. In fact, students must develop an international perspective and international skills if they are to participate as successful and productive citizens on behalf of their separate nations in the global environment. Students studying global education must view the United States as a partner with the rest of the countries of the world because their future depends on collaboration and understanding.

Some of the arguments by educators concerning the inclusion of global education into the curriculum have been more pragmatic in nature than philosophical. Teachers hesitate to include global issues in the curriculum for the following reasons:

- There is the perception that the curriculum is crowded and there is no room for additional topics or subjects. Teachers feel overwhelmed at the prospect of including in the curriculum only the topics for which they have national and state mandates. They feel there is not enough time in the school day to add additional subject matter.

- There is a lack of confidence in teaching about issues or regions of the world from which teachers may have had little or no formal training themselves. Few teachers have been presented a global curriculum in their teacher education programs and may feel incompetent to cover the material.
- There is limited access to high-quality curriculum resources that support global education. Some argue that there is a lack of time or funding to acquire the materials needed to teach a global curriculum.
- There are scarce resources for professional development. Instead, priorities have been placed on more pressing student needs.
- There is the belief that traditional subjects are critical, and although the philosophy behind global education is admirable, it is not necessary for students' success as they progress through their education programs and on to their careers.

It is impossible to avoid controversy when teaching international or global issues, but such controversy should be welcomed as an essential part of the learning process. Students should be taught to examine the many sides of complex global issues that all people of the world face. According to Schukar (1993), responsible citizenship demands that controversial issues not be set aside out of fear or discomfort. Teachers must learn not to fear such issues but rather to view them as natural to any system or institution that functions within a democratic society. Controversial issues need not be viewed as a negative, therefore, but rather as a positive means to the essential goal of preparing citizens for productive participation in the larger society.

Tye and Tye (1992) note that there are classrooms across the United States in which global education is not only taught but also embraced for the richness that it adds to the curriculum. For this to happen, however, they stress that the following conditions must be present:

- The student population must be ethnically diverse and from families interested in and actively supportive of the school.

- The faculty must consider diversity as a positive factor rather than as a problem and must be open to finding new ways to do their jobs better.
- Principals must be supportive, goal focused, and supportive of global education.
- The district/system administration must be supportive of global education and willing to defend the attacks on global curriculum by outside forces.
- The resources and materials to support the global curriculum must be available.

If global education is to be accepted as a regular part of the curriculum, teachers must put aside any personal hesitation they might have regarding teaching global issues. The need to present a global curriculum to the students of the twenty-first century means that teachers, administrators, politicians, and policymakers need to cross not only national borders and frontiers but mental ones as well. Pike (2000) agrees, stating, "If the meaning of global education is to be understood at a profound level, the challenge is to find creative ways to assist practitioners in the 'removal of national borders,' not just in their curriculum but also in their thinking" (p. 71).

THE NEED FOR THIS TEXTBOOK

If, as Tye and Tye (1992) state, global awareness will be the new basic skill of the twenty-first century, teachers must be given the skills necessary to successfully provide such a curriculum into their classroom. Le Roux (2001) agrees and stresses that all teachers need exposure to a global curriculum because of the following:

- Teachers who are exposed to a global curriculum appreciate the power and potential of being connected to other parts of the world.
- Teachers who are exposed to a global curriculum are more likely to find ways in their daily instruction to teach local/global interconnectedness.

- Teachers who are exposed to a global curriculum are able to construct bridges between their students' lives and the wider world.
- Teachers who are exposed to a global curriculum are more prepared to deal with diversity within the classroom.
- Teachers who are exposed to a global curriculum increase the depth and quality of what and how they teach.
- Teachers who are exposed to a global curriculum develop an appreciation of cultural differences and similarities, including ways to teach multiple perspectives and perspective consciousness.
- Teachers who are exposed to a global curriculum help students understand that local and personal decisions both affect and are affected by global connections, people, and organizations around the world.

Today's students live in an information society in which the newest telecommunication technologies provide instant access to the world. Knowledge is no longer circumscribed by national borders. Chapter 2 provides a framework for the integration of technology into the global curriculum. This framework is the International Society for Technology in Education's National Educational Technology Standards for Teachers. Each chapter in this book provides specific ideas and strategies for globalizing the classroom through technology.

Three models for globalizing the classroom are provided in chapters 3 to 5. Chapter 3 promotes a global curriculum that provides well-defined content focusing on understanding each other's differences and on reducing conflict between cultures. The elements of this global curriculum include the following:

- A study of problems and issues that cut across national boundaries
- The cultivation of cross-cultural understanding
- A study of the world community and the interdependency of its people and systems

Chapter 4 provides an integration approach to globalizing the curriculum. Global education is not a matter of simply adding foreign language courses or a unit on international relations, and it should not be restricted to social studies courses. Using the integration approach, teachers can incorporate global issues into all subject areas. Incorporating a global perspective does not require the creation of new courses but rather the integration of global education into the curriculum at all levels.

Chapter 5 presents the most traditional method of providing a global focus in the curriculum—the unit. According to Pike (2000), the focus of global education in the United States is more curriculum based and often provided within the context of a particular county or area. This method of instruction includes the study of a geographic region, the exploration of global science issues, and the contributions of books, music, and art from a particular country.

A global curriculum can and should be infused in all subject areas. It requires providing a global perspective for all curriculum areas, at all levels, including literature, the arts, the sciences, and the extracurricular experiences of students. The remaining chapters of this book provide strategies and methods for globalizing the curriculum with particular focus on the teaching of social studies, science, literature, mathematics, and the related arts (physical education, art, music, and drama).

REFERENCES

Chanda, J. (1992). Multicultural education and the visual arts. *Arts Education Policy Review, 94,* 12–17.

Gilliom, M. E. (1981). Global education and the social studies. *Theory into Practice, 20,* 169–173.

Hanvey, R. G. (1975). *An attainable global perspective.* New York: Center for War/Peace Studies.

Hendrix, J. C. (1998). Globalizing the curriculum. *Clearing House, 71,* 305–308.

Kirkwood, T. F. (2001). Global age requires global education: Clarifying definitional ambiguities. *The Social Studies, 92,* 10–15.

Le Roux, J. (2001). Re-examining global education's relevance beyond 2000. *Research in Education, 65,* 70–81.

Merryfield, M. M. (1995). *Teacher education in global and international education* Washington, DC: ERIC Clearinghouse on Teaching and Teacher Education. (ERIC Document Reproduction Service No. ED384601.)

Merryfield, M. M. (1997). A framework for teachers preparing teachers to teach global perspectives. In M. M. Merryfield, E. Jachow, & S. Pickert (Eds.), *Preparing teachers to teach global perspectives: A handbook for teacher educators* (pp. 1–25). Thousand Oaks, CA: Corwin Press.

Pike, G. (2000). Global education and national identity: In pursuit of meaning. *Theory into Practice, 39,* 64–73.

Ramler, S. (1991). Global education for the 21st century. *Educational Leadership, 48,* 44–47.

Schukar, R. (1993). Controversy in global education: Lessons for teacher educators. *Theory into Practice, 32,* 52–57.

Tye, B. B., & Tye, K. A. (1990). *Global education: From thought to action. The 1991 ASCD Yearbook.* Alexandria, VA: Association for Supervision and Curriculum Development.

Tye, B. B., & Tye, K. A. (1992). *Global education: A study of school change.* Albany: State University of New York Press.

Tye, K. A. (2003). Global education as a worldwide movement. *Phi Delta Kappan, 85,* 165–168.

CHAPTER 2

Globalization and Technology

The new electronic interdependence recreates the world in the image of a global village.

—Marshall McLuhan, p. 31 of McLuhan, M. (1962). *The Gutenberg Galaxy*. London: Routledge & Kegan Paul

Chapter 1 introduced the philosophy of a global curriculum and stressed the importance of an educational process that promotes understanding the contributions and customs of all cultures. Until recently, however, the resources have not been in place to fully implement such a process, and educators have not had what they needed to create multicultural learning experiences for their students. The concept of global education was introduced almost fifty years ago, but only in recent years has the technology progressed sufficiently to make the concept a reality. As schools continue to purchase computers, place them in learning environments, and provide Internet connectivity, teachers discover the innumerable possibilities for connecting their students with the rest of the world.

This union of the global education philosophy and the capability to communicate and share information worldwide now provides students with the tools necessary to successfully participate in the twenty-first century. Canadian literary critic Marshall McLuhan first conceptualized the vision of this particular union when he coined the phrase "global village" in 1960. Although McLuhan believed that the technology of telephones and television would lead to globalization, in a 1965 television interview he predicted that, in the future, people not only would no longer gather in classrooms to learn but would be able to move anywhere through "electronic circuitry" (Canadian Broadcasting Corporation, 2004). Forty years later, students are learning and communicating precisely as he envisioned.

Prior to the technological advances of the past century, students learned from books in a solitary, linear fashion. Learners received new information as they read books, and those without access to books or teachers had little hope of learning more. Computer technology, in particular the Internet, allows all learners to get information simultaneously. McLuhan refers to this phenomenon as "tribal learning" as opposed to individual learning (Canadian Broadcasting Corporation, 2004). His global village metaphor brings to mind a picture of a small, intimate community where neighbors are friendly and work together for the common good. Students of today will become the global villagers of the future and find it imperative to have the tools and background to become active participants.

The technological advances of the past decade and the increasing availability of computers and Internet access create fertile soil for the roots of global education in today's classrooms. Current technology allows students throughout the world to participate in learning activities, share multimedia presentations, and communicate electronically with others. Students and educators have instant access to the vast body of information available today on the Internet. The 2002 Digest of Educational Statistics reports that 99 percent of all public schools in the United States have Internet access and that 87 percent of all instructional classrooms have computers with online capabilities (National Center for Education Statistics, 2002). With the necessary hardware already in place, it is now possible for teachers to plant the seeds of global awareness.

Internet access has provided opportunities for communication across national borders, allowing people from different cultures to share ideas, solve problems, and become friends. Time-consuming mail correspondence and expensive long-distance phone bills are no longer obstacles to connecting with others around the world. Boundaries such as these once prevented students from discovering much more about other cultures than they could by reading social studies textbooks and encyclopedias. The material they found was sometimes out of date and often emphasized the differences between countries and cultures rather than the similarities. Internet access to information about other parts of the world takes much of the enigma away from faraway countries and allows students and teachers to feel like a part of the global village. Today, Internet-savvy students can discover more about the people and cultures of other nations through communicating in real-time chat rooms, taking virtual field trips, accessing detailed databases, and participating in global group projects.

As educators continue to develop their abilities to integrate technology in the teaching and learning process, they can create learning experiences that enable their students to feel they are part of the global community. With each new generation of personal computers and the accompanying peripherals, students in the United States and other developed countries have easier access to the Internet and communication with others around the world. While this may not be true for students in other parts of the world where significantly less access exists to technology, even the most remote areas of the earth are making progress toward this goal.

Although the difference in technology access between developed and developing countries, often referred to as the digital divide, is an obstacle to the benefits of information technology, organizations such as the United Nations have committed to providing aid to the less advantaged countries. A press release of the UN's 58th General Assembly reported that "the advent of information and communication technologies has fostered economic growth, sustainable development, and poverty eradication in some nations" (United Nations, 2003). Internet connectivity is finally reaching even the most isolated areas of the earth. The World Factbook (2003) published by the Central Intelligence Agency reports that all but 11 of the 268 countries in the world have at least one Internet service provider, indicating that Internet service is available at some level within each of those countries. As access to technology improves, opportunities for global learning experiences increase.

STANDARDS AND STRATEGIES

The use of technology in classrooms creates new challenges for educators, and determining how and when students use computers for learning activities is a subject of much debate. The International Society for Technology in Education (ISTE) is an organization dedicated to providing leadership and service to improve teaching and learning by advancing the effective use of technology in K–12 education and teacher education (ISTE, 2004). In addition to advocating technology integration in education, ISTE collaborates with other educators and organizations to identify and apply the best practices in teaching and learning. It also provides a variety of resources for students, teachers, and administrators, including detailed technology performance standards for these three groups.

The ISTE's National Educational Technology Standards (NETS) became available for students in 1998, for teachers in 2000, and for administrators in 2001. The National Council for the Accreditation for Teacher Education has adopted these standards in its requirements for teacher education programs. The departments of education of all fifty states and the District of Columbia have adopted, adapted, referenced, or aligned with the ISTE standards in their expectations for educators.

The ISTE's National Educational Technology Standards for Students (NETS-S) are separated into six broad categories that are to be introduced, reinforced, and achieved by students throughout their pre-K–12 educational experiences. To meet the challenges of the future, NETS-S grounds its philosophy in the belief that the world is changing in ways that require a changing learning environment to prepare students to meet the challenges of the future. Educators use these six categories of standards to serve as guidelines for creating and implementing technology-based learning experiences. Additionally, forty-two states make reference to the standards in their technology plans.

Based on the NETS for Students, the National Educational Technology Standards for Teachers (NETS-T) provide goals and guidelines for teachers' technology skills (see Table 2.1). The standards are specific enough to be measurable and flexible so that they can be customized to fit state and local guidelines. Teachers who master these standards have

Table 2.1   National Educational Technology Standards for Teachers (NETS-T).

Technology operations and concepts
Teachers demonstrate a sound understanding of technology operations and concepts. They:
• demonstrate introductory knowledge, skills, and understanding of concepts related to technology (as described in the ISTE National Education Technology Standards for Students).
• demonstrate continual growth in technology knowledge and skills to stay abreast of current and emerging technologies.

Planning and designing learning environments and experiences
Teachers plan and design effective learning environments and experiences supported by technology. They:
- design developmentally appropriate learning opportunities that apply technology-enhanced instructional strategies to support the diverse needs of learners.
- apply current research on teaching and learning with technology when planning learning environments and experiences.
- identify and locate technology resources and evaluate them for accuracy and suitability.
- plan for the management of technology resources within the context of learning activities.
- plan strategies to manage student learning in a technology-enhanced environment.

Teaching, learning, and the curriculum
Teachers implement curriculum plans that include methods and strategies for applying technology to maximize student learning. They:
- facilitate technology-enhanced experiences that address content standards and student technology standards.
- use technology to support learner-centered strategies that address the diverse needs of students.
- apply technology to develop students' higher-order skills and creativity.
- manage student learning activities in a technology-enhanced environment.

Assessment and evaluation
Teachers apply technology to facilitate a variety of effective assessment and evaluation strategies. They:
- apply technology in assessing student learning of subject matter using a variety of assessment techniques.
- use technology resources to collect and analyze data, interpret results, and communicate findings to improve instructional practice and maximize student learning.
- apply multiple methods of evaluation to determine students' appropriate use of technology resources for learning, communication, and productivity.
- apply technology in assessing student learning of subject matter using a variety of assessment techniques.

Productivity and professional practice
Teachers use technology to enhance their productivity and professional practice. They:
- use technology resources to engage in ongoing professional development and lifelong learning.
- continually evaluate and reflect on professional practice to make informed decisions regarding the use of technology in support of student learning.
- apply technology to increase productivity.
- use technology to communicate and collaborate with peers, parents, and the larger community in order to nurture student learning.

Social, ethical, legal, and human issues
Teachers understand the social, ethical, legal, and human issues surrounding the use of technology in preK–12 schools and apply those principles in practice. They:
- model and teach legal and ethical practice related to technology use.
- apply technology resources to enable and empower learners with diverse backgrounds, characteristics, and abilities.
- identify and use technology resources that affirm diversity.
- promote safe and healthy use of technology resources.
- facilitate equitable access to technology resources for all students.

a high degree of knowledge about the concepts and skills necessary for technology integration in the classroom as well as positive attitudes toward using computers as tools for teaching and learning.

In the *NETS for Teachers* handbook, ISTE identifies four model strategies proven effective for integrating technology across all disciplines and in a variety of educational situations (ISTE, 2002). These strategies are generic enough to integrate well with a wide variety of global education experiences. The learning activities suggested throughout this book address both the student and the teacher standards and are examples of the four model strategies, which include the following:

- Web-based lessons
- Multimedia presentations
- Telecomputing projects
- Online discussions

WEB-BASED LESSONS

The first model strategy identified in ISTE's *NETS for Teachers* is the Web-based lesson. This is an activity that includes the Internet as a critical component of the learning experience. A primary example of a Web-based lesson is the WebQuest, an Internet-based teaching technique developed by Bernie Dodge and Tom March at San Diego State University in 1995. The WebQuest is an inquiry-oriented activity in which most or all of the information used by learners is drawn from the Internet. A WebQuest presents student groups with a challenging task, scenario, or problem to solve. Successful WebQuests involve topics that are under dispute or that require students to look at several different perspectives of a pertinent issue. Current events and controversial social and environmental issues work well, as do topics that require evaluation and that evoke a variety of interpretations. The Internet is an excellent tool for this type of learning activity because it offers the breadth of perspectives and viewpoints that are usually needed to construct meaning on complex topics. Students benefit from linking to a wide variety of Internet resources through which they can explore and make sense of the issues involved in the challenge.

Although WebQuests have become familiar learning activities for many teachers, other types of Web-based lessons are also highly effective. An example is CyberGuides, which are supplementary, standards-based, Web-delivered units of instruction centered on core works of literature (Schools of California Online Resources for Education, n.d.). Students work through a series of tasks dealing with the subject matter of a novel they are reading. These supplemental tasks use Internet resources to help students gain a clearer understanding of the elements of the story. Although all CyberGuides are literature based, many deal with global topics.

A third example of a Web-based lesson model is Filamentality, a website that provides templates and resources that allow educators to create their own Internet-based activity or search for one to modify to match their curricular objectives. Templates for several different types of Web-based activities are available at this site. The fill-in-the-blank style is user friendly, and teachers can create activities in the following formats:

- Hotlists are Web pages that link to the locations of specific websites to be used in support of a learning activity. This saves the learner time searching for appropriate sites and focuses on the content of the preselected sites.
- Scrapbooks are Web pages containing a collection of Internet sites organized around specific categories, such as photographs, maps, stories, facts, quotations, sound clips, videos, and virtual reality tours. Learners use the Scrapbook to find aspects of the broader topic that they feel are important. Then they download or copy and paste these scraps into a variety of formats: newsletter, desktop slide presentation, collage, bulletin board, HyperStudio stack, or Web page.
- Treasure Hunts are activities to use when developing some solid factual knowledge on a subject. The strategy here is to find Web pages that hold information (text, graphics, sound, video, and so on) essential to understanding the given topic. Treasure Hunts consist of ten to fifteen links that pose one key question for each Web resource. When a culminating question is included, students can synthesize what they have learned and shape it into a broader understanding of the larger picture.

- Subject Samplers present a smaller number of intriguing websites organized around a main topic. Rather than uncover facts as they do in a Treasure Hunt, students consider 1) their perspectives on topics, 2) similarities to experiences they have had, or 3) interpretations of art works or data. More important than the right answer is that students are invited to join the community of learners surrounding the topic to see that their views are valued in this context. The strong advantage of using Subject Samplers is that they can make students feel connected to the topic and that the subject matter is meaningful.
- Filamentality also includes a template for WebQuests. This template allows teachers to quickly and easily create a WebQuest from their preselected Internet sites. In addition to creating original Web-Quests, hundreds of existing WebQuests created with Filamentality are available for modification or adaptation at the site.

When teachers create their own Web-based lessons using Filamentality, they can personalize the resources and content to specifically match the topic they want to teach. After the activity is complete and posted to the Web with a unique address, it is accessible from any computer with Internet access. Teachers may go back at any time and change and update their Web-based lessons with Filamentality's easy-to-use site.

MULTIMEDIA PRESENTATIONS

The ISTE identifies multimedia presentations as another highly effective method of integrating technology into the curriculum. Multimedia projects combine a variety of media, such as text, graphics, video, photographs, animation, and sound into an integrated, meaningful package.

When teachers assign multimedia projects, students master the content as they select the types of media that they feel best conveys the information. The use of technology to present the results of research is a motivational learning experience for many students. New knowledge and skills emerge as students go through the process of designing, planning, and producing a multimedia project.

Examples of multimedia projects include creating a Web page or site, developing a branching hypermedia stack, using PowerPoint or a similar multimedia tool to create a computer presentation, and editing digital video to create a computer-generated movie. Exemplary multimedia projects include several criteria. They are multidisciplinary, anchored in core curriculum, demonstrate sustained effort over time, promote student decision making, support collaborative guesswork, exhibit a real-world connection, utilize systematic assessment, and employ multimedia as a communication tool (ISTE, 2002).

One example of an effective use of multimedia presentations is Inter national Schools CyberFair. This award-winning learning program is used by schools and youth organizations around the world. Sponsored by the Global Schoolhouse, this contest requires participants to conduct research and publish their findings on the Internet in the form of multimedia presentations. The best projects receive recognition in one of eight categories: local leaders, businesses, community organizations, historical landmarks, environment, music, art, or local specialties. CyberFair encourages youth to connect the knowledge they learn in school to real-world applications, and the best projects showcase people and programs that are actively providing solutions or solving problems.

ThinkQuest is a semiannual international competition where student teams engage in collaborative, project-based learning to create educational websites. The model provides opportunities for students in grades 4 through 12 to collaborate on projects. This White House–endorsed program encourages youths to become community ambassadors by working collaboratively and using technology to share what they have learned. A searchable library hosts more than 5,000 submitted projects, and teachers and learners can explore a multitude of topics and brainstorm ideas for developing their own multimedia projects.

TELECOMPUTING PROJECTS

A third model strategy identified by ISTE (2002) involves participation in projects with other students around the world. Telecomputing projects are Internet-enriched learning activities that often involve students in one location collaborating with students or adults in one or more other locations. Online resources include websites and interactive environments. Judi Harris at the College of William and Mary has researched and studied telecomputing projects for more than fifteen years and has determined that the projects focus on at least one of three primary learning processes: interpersonal exchange, information collection and analysis, or problem solving.

Interpersonal exchange activities involve students or groups of students who communicate with each other electronically through e-mail, chat rooms, bulletin boards, or audio- and videoconferencing. These activities include learning situations that require student-to-student communication, group-to-group communication, or electronic contact with an expert or specialist in a particular area. Information collection and analysis activities ask students to collaborate with other students locally or globally to collect, compile, and compare different types of information. Problem-solving activities are important learning experiences for students, and the Internet provides a valuable resource for information. Examples of problem-solving learning experiences include information searches, peer feedback activities, parallel problem solving, simulations, and social action projects (Harris, 1998).

Harris (1999) has also identified the following specific learning activities, or student action sequences, that have been successful in other telecomputing projects used by teachers in their classrooms:

Correspond: Prepare a communication locally and send it to others. They respond, and the process continues.

Compete: Register to participate in an Internet activity and then do the activity locally. Submit completed work by a deadline and receive feedback.

Comprehend: Locate online resources and then make primarily local use of them.

Collect, share, and compare: Create something locally and add it to a group of similarly created works from other locales at a central online location.

Chain: Do an activity locally, create records of that activity, and send something on so that the next group can do something similar.

Come along: Using the Internet, students follow the experiences of others as they travel either physically or cognitively, perhaps communicating briefly in the process.

Collaborate: Work with others at a remote location to realize a common goal.

Teachers can access current telecomputing projects at the Virtual Architecture Web Home (Harris, 1999). The Internet Projects Registry also provides teachers with opportunities to participate in telecomputing projects and has a searchable database that describes more than 1,000 available projects.

ONLINE DISCUSSIONS

The ISTE (2002) identifies online discussions as another type of exemplary learning activity. With the growth of connectedness around the world comes the ability to access others through remote connections. Students and teachers can connect to experts and peers through a variety of formats, such as chat rooms, electronic bulletin boards, and e mail. Asynchronous communication allows participants to send and receive information at times suitable to their schedule. This also allows time for reflection before responding. Synchronous communication, however, is real-time online communication and provides immediate feedback for reinforcement and understanding. Several commercial programs, such as Blackboard and WebCT, support online environments that allow the posting of class materials as well as chat and threaded discussions with password protection.

An example of online discussion for teachers is Tapped In. This website brings educators together both locally and globally to develop a community that supports each teacher as a professional. In addition, it builds the capacity of teachers to support one another through peer networks supported by the Tapped In community. Educators can join this website and participate in the following:

- Plan and conduct learning projects with colleagues and students
- Participate in or lead topical discussion and groups
- Manage and attend online courses offered by Tapped In providers
- Mentor other educators
- Try out new ideas in a safe, supportive environment

Each of the four models for technology integration aligns with the philosophy of developing a global curriculum. In the following chapters, specific examples are given for using these effective models within the global education, integration, and focused unit approaches. Additionally, ideas are suggested for using these models in the social studies, science, mathematics, literature, related arts, and physical education curricula. Teachers may find links to specific activities on the textbook website, or they can create original global learning experiences for their students.

INSTRUCTIONAL IDEAS

Web-Based Lessons

WebQuests are popular learning activities for students and teachers. An example of a WebQuest with a global focus is the Big Wide World WebQuest. The goal of this lesson is to help students understand how all aspects of the world work together.

With partners, students use preselected Internet resources to become an expert on one of the Windows on the World, which include the globe, plants, animals, people, cultures, and language. After researching a particular topic, the students collaborate to create a set of rules that pertain to their area of expertise.

Then students get together in groups with at least one representative from each Window on the World. Using a relationship wheel, students compare the rules they created and try to determine how each of the topics relates to each other.

The large group must then come to a consensus on an answer to the question, What about this big wide world, how does it all work? A scoring rubric evaluates the students' individual research, their group's conclusion, and how well they worked together.

Multimedia Projects

Multimedia projects created for the International Schools Cyberfair require students to use many types of media when creating the project website. Digital photographs, graphics, video, and audio are just a few of the media component students use to do so.

An example of a Cyberfair multimedia project is Our River, Our Dream—the Chien-Chen River, created by students at Kaohsiung Municipal Hsing Jen Junior High School in Kaohsiung, Taiwan. The students' goal was to research the history of the once clear and beautiful Chien-Chen River that runs through their community. Their dream is to see the river's water clear and transparent once again so that the fish will return. Through interviews, photographs, drawings, and video, the students have created an online history of the Chien-Chen River. While the creation of a Cyberfair site is a valuable learning experience for the participating students, existing sites can be used by any students to gather information and learn more about other cultures.

Telecomputing Projects

Among the earliest instructional uses of technology were telecomputing projects, such as Internet-enriched activities that involve students in one location collaborating with students or adults in one or more other locations. While these projects can take on many different forms, a popular model is one where students collect information in their community and share and compare it with students in other locales.

An example of this type of project is the Global Grocery List, a long-standing project that generates real, peer-collected data for student computation, analysis, and conclusion building within the context of social studies, science, mathematics, and other disciplines.

Students participating in the Global Grocery List project go to the grocery store and collect the prices of common items on the list from the website. All students in the class report their findings, and the class results are averaged and submitted to the site. Lesson strategies for using the resulting data are available on the website and include averaging numbers, determining correlation, using spreadsheets, and predicting outcomes.

Online Discussions

One of the resources available for educators at the Peace Corps website is the CyberVolunteers Program. CyberVolunteers are current Peace Corps Volunteers who wish to share their experiences with American students through letters sent from the field.

Participants receive two letters each month, one for elementary students and one for secondary students. Each letter is accompanied by lesson plans to help teachers integrate the letter into their classroom activities. The letters can be integrated throughout the curriculum and include such topics as the importance of language in our culture, what can be learned about a culture from its folktales, how the lack of consumer goods affects people's lives, and how the introduction of technology can affect traditional culture.

The CyberVolunteer program is an effective tool for transferring knowledge across cultural and national borders and educating students about the environmental, social, cultural, and political surroundings in which volunteers work.

INTERNET RESOURCES

The Big Wide World WebQuest: http://www.kn.pacbell.com/wired/bww/index.html

Blackboard: http://www.blackboard.com

CyberFair: http://www.gsn.org/cf/

Cyberguides: http://www.sdcoe.k12.ca.us/score/cyberguide.html

Filamentality: http://www.kn.pacbell.com/wired/fil/

Global Grocery List: http://www.landmark-project.com/ggl/

Global Schoolhouse: http://www.globalschoolnet.org/GSH/

Internet Projects Registry: http://www.globalschoolhouse.org/pr/_cfm/index.cfm

ISTE: http://iste.org

ISTE NETS-S: http://cnets.iste.org/students/s_book.html

ISTE NETS-T: http://cnets.iste.org/teachers/index.shtml

Our River, Our Dream—the Chien-Chen River: http://gsh.taiwanschoolnet.org/gsh2004/3263/index.htm

Peace Corps: http://www.peacecorps.gov/wws/educators/index.html

Tapped In: http://www.tappedin.org/

ThinkQuest: http://www.thinkquest.org/

Virtual Architecture Web Home: http://virtual-architecture.wm.edu/

WebCT: http://www.webct.com/

WebQuests: http://webquest.org

REFERENCES

Canadian Broadcasting Corporation. (2004). *Marshall McLuhan, the man and his message.* Retrieved from http://archives.cbc.ca/IDD-1-74-342/people/mcluhan/

Harris, J. (1998). Activity structures for curriculum-based telecollaboration. *Learning and Leading with Technology, 26*(1), 6–15.

Harris, J. (1999). "I know what we're doing but how do we do it?" Action sequences for curriculum based telecomputing. *Learning and Leading with Technology, 26*(6), 42–44.

International Society for Technology in Education. (2002). *NETS for teachers— Preparing teachers to use technology.* Retrieved from http://cnets.iste.org/teachers/pdf/Sec_1-3_Model_Strategies.pdf

International Society for Technology in Education. (2004). Retrieved from http://www.iste.org/

National Center for Education Statistics. (2002). *Internet access in U.S. public schools, fall 2002.* Retrieved from http://nces.ed.gov/surveys/frss/publications/2004011/2.asp

Schools of California Online Resources for Education. (n.d). Retrieved from http://www.sdcoe.k12.ca.us/SCORE/cyberguide.html

United Nations. (2003, November). Unequal benefits of globalization, need to implement development financing commitments focus of second committee debate. Press Release GA/EF/3065. Retrieved from http://www.un.org/News/Press/docs/2003/gaef3065.doc.htm

World Factbook. (2003). Retrieved from http://www.odci.gov/cia/publications/factbook/fields/2152.html

THREE APPROACHES TO GLOBALIZING THE CURRICULUM

Part 2 of this book presents three models for globalizing the classroom. Chapter 3 promotes a global curriculum that provides well-defined content and focuses on understanding each other's differences and on reducing conflict between cultures. Chapter 4 provides an integration approach to globalizing the curriculum. Using the integration approach, teachers should incorporate global issues into all subject areas. Incorporating a global perspective does not require the creation of new courses but rather the integration of global education into the curriculum at all levels. Chapter 5 presents the most traditional method of providing a global focus in the curriculum—the unit method. This method of instruction includes the study of a geographic region, the exploration of global science issues, or the contributions through books, music, and art from a particular country.

CHAPTER 3

Global Education

When we form meaningful relationships with our friends around
the world, we can work together and cooperate with one another to
eliminate ignorance, hatred, and violence.

—Rod Paige, former secretary of education, Oct. 27, 2004,
statement for *National Education Week*
(http://exchanges.state.gov/iew/statements/paige.htm)

Today's teachers face a multitude of curricular choices as they prepare
students for a new focus on standards-based education. A major decision
involves how to include global issues in the curriculum. Many would argue that there is no room in an already crowded curriculum for the inclusion of global issues. They would suggest that global issues be integrated into the existing curriculum or scattered throughout the year
through units in social studies focusing on particular countries. Others
argue that the teaching of global issues is as critical as the teaching of language arts, mathematics, social studies, and science and therefore should
be added as a separate curriculum and a planned part of instruction.

Global education should be seen as a solution to help solve many of
the problems we face as human beings. When done properly, global education promotes critical thinking, as it encourages students to find creative solutions to new and challenging situations. It is hoped that
through global education, students will take action in eliminating
global oppression and inequity. Global education programs prepare students for citizenship in a world where the economic, political, social,
and cultural connections between nations increase daily.

If global education is not part of the established curriculum, students will not be prepared for participation in an increasingly complex and interconnected world. Global cooperation is necessary for economic purposes, as an understanding of a global economy will be necessary whether a student is buying a personal item over the Internet or running a major corporation. But more important, global education is necessary to prepare our students to respond appropriately to global environmental problems, such as population increases, food and energy shortages, pollution, economic and monetary issues, and problems associated with the development process of lesser-developed countries.

Gilliom (1981) suggests that a global curriculum is especially critical for students in the United States. He stresses that many students in the United States have a myopic view of the world and see all issues only as they relate to the needs of American citizens. Teachers who present a global education strive to reduce this cultural myopia by helping students deal with the world as an interconnected, global web in which all people share a common history and a common destiny. Although global education recognizes the importance of commonalities among humankind, it also is concerned with the differences among peoples and nations. A person with a global perspective recognizes that all people are members of a single species, enriched by diversity.

There are many definitions of global education, but in essence it can be defined as those educational efforts designed to cultivate in young people a global perspective and to develop the knowledge, skills, and attitudes needed to live effectively in a modern world. Global education strives to help students recognize that other cultures possess unique value systems, different frames of reference, different modes of thought and action, and different worldviews. However, recognition is not enough. Global education focuses on the acceptance of these differences. Students who develop an understanding of, appreciation for, and acceptance of these differences have the foundations of a global perspective.

Tye and Tye (1992) define a global curriculum in the following ways:

- It is a curriculum that engages students of all ages and in all subject matters in the study of humankind.

- It is a curriculum that engages students in the study of the earth as humankind's home.
- It is a curriculum that engages students in the study of global systems and human organizations.
- It is a curriculum that engages students in the study of themselves as members of the human species, as inhabitants of planet earth, and as participants of the social order.

GOALS OF A GLOBAL CURRICULUM

To determine the direction global education will take in a particular school or classroom, it is important to determine the goals to be accomplished by incorporating a global curriculum. Such goals might include the following:

- Providing students with an expanded vision of citizenship. Through global education, students learn to view themselves as citizens in the global community.
- Helping students recognize and appreciate the complexity and constantly changing nature of the world's political, economic, and social systems.
- Creating an understanding and appreciation of basic human commonalities and differences. Through global education, students learn how different cultures organize their respective systems to acquire the basic human needs of food, shelter, clothing, health care, and education. The emphasis is on the similarities and differences between individuals, groups, organizations, and nations.
- Developing an awareness of how perceptions, values, and priorities differ among various individuals, groups, organizations, and cultures. The emphasis is on how perceptions and values influence individual and group decision making.

COMPONENTS OF A GLOBAL CURRICULUM

Many have suggested what concepts should be included in a comprehensive global curriculum. Merryfield (1995, 1997) has expanded on the work of Hanvey (1975), Hendrix (1998), and Kniep (1986) to develop what is clearly the most inclusive model of a comprehensive global curriculum.

The eight components of Merryfield's model can be divided into two groups. Components 1 to 4 provide the students the substantive knowledge needed to develop a global perspective that is the foundation of global education. This includes knowledge of world events, states of affairs, places, and concepts students must understand in order to develop a world perspective.

Components 5 to 8 are designed to create learning environments and opportunities that allow for the development of a global perspective by reducing prejudices, stereotyping, and ethnocentrism. The elements of components 5 to 8 promote concepts, orientations, values, sensibilities, and attitudes needed by students in order to be accepting of those different from themselves. Global education's purpose goes beyond the acquisition of knowledge about the world and includes skills and attitudinal development. Components 5 to 8 promote this purpose. Merryfield's eight components of global education are outlined in Table 3.1.

Table 3.1   Merryfield's Elements of Global Education. Source: Merryfield (1995, 1997).

Components 1–4	Components 5–8
Elements focusing on the substantive dimensions of global education	Elements focusing on the perspective dimensions of global education
The Study of Human and Universal Values	The Study of Cross-Cultural Understanding and Interaction
The Study of Global Systems	Awareness of Human Choices
The Study of Global Issues and Problems	Development of Analytical and Evaluative Skills
The Study of Global History	Strategies for Participation and Involvement

Component 1: The Study of Human and Universal Values

The first component of Merryfield's model deals with the study of human and universal values and is designed to help students perceive the qualities of humanness shared with those different from them. Merryfield (1997) includes the following elements:

- Universal and diverse human beliefs and values
- Perspective consciousness/multiple perspectives
- Recognition of the effects of one's own values, culture, and world-view in learning about and interacting with people different from oneself
- An understanding of how values and beliefs underlie social/cultural norms and human conflict
- The role of human beliefs and values in aesthetics; in language, literature, and oral traditions; in the use of natural resources and the environment; in technology; in governance; and in the construction of history

Essential to this component is a review of human values. This review involves both personal values and values common to all human beings. As students come to understand their own personal values, they realize that their values are shaped by their experiences and that their values determine how they view the world and influence their decisions and behaviors.

Through global education, students come to understand that their values are typically shared with their own ethnic, national, and religious groups but may differ greatly from those whose backgrounds are unlike theirs.

Global education is concerned primarily with the universal human values that transcend group identity. A global curriculum must be proactive and include learning experiences that promote the adoption of values conducive to a sense of justice and equality for all individuals. These universal values are best exemplified through the United Nations Universal Declaration of Human Rights. Created in 1948, the Universal Declaration of Human Rights maintains that all human beings are entitled to life, liberty, property, equality, justice, freedom of religion, free speech, peaceful assembly, and asylums, and it outlaws slavery, torture, and arbitrary imprisonment or detention. These universal values have their origins in a variety of cultural, religious, and national traditions. Through global education, students come to understand that all humans are entitled to certain rights and privileges simply because they are human.

To adopt values different from their own, students must develop what Hanvey (1975) describes as perspective consciousness. Perspective consciousness is the recognition that one's own values may not be universally shared. Perspective consciousness is generally interpreted to mean the provision of insights, ideas, and information that enables students to look beyond the confines of local and national boundaries in their thinking and aspirations. Merryfield (1997) describes perspective consciousness as an identifying characteristic of global education.

Essential to perspective consciousness is the concept of multiple perspectives, which encourages students to consider differing views on any issue before reaching a judgment. The ability to see one's world both from the mainstream and from those marginalized in society is a shared characteristic of multicultural and global education. Students, therefore, must be exposed to individuals who, because of their race, gender, class, culture, national origin, or religious or political beliefs, are ignored, stereotyped, or marginalized in society (Merryfield, 2001). This interaction will often create uncomfortable moments, and McCabe (1997) warns that students often experience "cognitive confrontation" or "cultural shock" as they question the personal values once considered sacred.

Component 2: The Study of Global Systems

It is important for students to understand the complexity of the systems connecting the people of the world. Now, more than anytime in human history, people across the world share interacting political, economic, technological, and ecological systems. These interacting systems create issues that can no longer be addressed by individual nations. To help students understand this interdependence, global education programs must provide them with opportunities to study global systems. The study of global systems proposed by Merryfield (1995) includes the following:

- Economic systems
- Political systems
- Ecological systems
- Technological systems (including information, communication, transportation, and manufacturing)
- Knowledge of global dynamics

- Procedures and mechanisms in global systems
- Transactions within and across peoples, nations, and regions
- Interconnections within different global systems
- State-of-the-planet awareness

Although worldwide systems are certainly not new, the magnitude and scope of their interdependence has increased radically in the past fifty years. This increase in interdependence is due partly to advances in science and technology. Constant change in the political makeup of the world, along with the creation and involvement of the United Nations, has also contributed to this interdependence. All people, regardless of where or how they live, now function daily in a number of interacting global systems, and this global interdependence will only increase in the future.

It will be impossible, therefore, to shelter students from the threat or promise of such interdependence. To be ready for the world ahead, students must be able to understand the historical development and current trends of global systems and to understand the nature of economic, political, ecological, and technological systems (Merryfield, 1991).

Economic Systems

A global education must help students see themselves as participants within a global economy. The global economic system is primarily a capitalistic, market economy in which activity is profit driven. Decisions regarding what should be produced affect all of society. This interdependent economic system includes issues concerning the world's workforce, monetary values, and interest rates. Because students will participate in the global economic system as both consumers and producers, they must understand the economic linkage from themselves to others around the world.

Political Systems

Opportunities for participation in world political affairs have escalated dramatically since World War II. As people move from the concept of citizens of a state or nation, they seek to be actively involved in the decisions made worldwide. Students need to understand how political changes across the world affect their lives and that they, in turn, have an opportunity to affect the lives of others by taking stands on political issues such as wealth and poverty, power and oppression, peace and conflict, human rights, and injustice.

Ecological Systems

The world environment is characterized by finite natural resources that must be shared by all living creatures. Because the earth's complex ecological system is radically affected by human activities, it is important for students to understand their role in protecting the earth and its people. They must come to an understanding that they have the power to manage, maintain, exploit, or destroy the earth. Global education teaches students the interdependent and symbiotic relationship of living and nonliving things and the special role human beings play in ecological systems.

Technological Systems

Perhaps the most significant development of the twentieth century was the accelerated development of technology. Modern technologies are transforming the way individuals live, work, and relate to one another and their environment. Two advances in technology—transportation and communication—have had the most profound impact on society. These advances are quickly shrinking our world in terms of the time it takes to cover distances and enlarging our world in terms of the amount of information available. These advances provide students an opportunity to have a personal relationship with students from every part of the world.

Component 3: The Study of Global Issues and Problems

Students must engage in discussions and projects about the causes, effects, and solutions to global issues and problems. Kniep (1986) suggests that critical global issues share five characteristics:

1. The issues and problems are transnational.
2. The problems cannot be solved by one nation alone.

3. Conflict is inherent in the problems.
4. The problems and issues have developed over many years and are likely to persist in some form in the future.
5. The problems are linked to one another.

The third component of the global curriculum deals with the study of these global issues and problems and includes the following elements:

- Population and family issues
- Self-determination
- Human rights issues (including rights of women, indigenous peoples, and children)
- Emigration, immigration, and refugees
- Global commons
- Environmental/natural resource issues
- Issues related to distribution of wealth, technology and information, resources, and access to markets
- Issues related to hunger and food
- Peace and security issues
- Issues related to prejudice and discrimination (Merryfield, 1995)

Many of these issues overlap and can be viewed as primarily political or environmental. Issues of wealth and poverty, power and oppression, peace and conflict, human rights, injustice, and inequality all have political undertones. The study of development issues engages students in the struggles of peoples and nations to meet their basic needs, achieve national economic growth, and expand their political power.

Environmental issues often fall under what Case (1993) calls "state of the planet awareness." This includes the knowledge of prevailing and emergent world conditions, including population growth, migration, economic conditions, natural resources, the physical environment, political developments, science and technology, law, health, and international and intranational conflicts.

A global education program should allow students to understand their roles in developing solutions to global issues and problems. They must be given opportunities to grapple with general categories of content, such as peace and security issues, developmental issues, environmental issues, and human rights issues. These global issues will not be resolved without deliberate action on the part of citizens who understand the complexities of the issues. Unfortunately, it will be the responsibility of the next generation to solve many of the problems created by our generation.

Component 4: The Study of Global History

The elements of component 4 clearly support the other seven components of Merryfield's model. As Merryfield (1995) notes, students must have substantive knowledge in order to develop the global perspective needed to change the world. This substantive knowledge includes a historical perspective of today's world. For a true understanding of the events that have brought humanity to this point in time, global history must include a grasp of the evolution of universal and diverse human values, the historical development of our contemporary global systems, and the antecedent conditions and causes of today's global issues and problems. Unfortunately, many courses in world history do little to help students understand global issues and problems because they emphasize only the histories of Western civilizations.

Merryfield (1995) suggests that a study of global history must include the following:

- Acceleration of interdependence over time
- Antecedents to current issues
- Origins and development of cultures
- Contact and borrowing among cultures
- Evolution of global systems
- Conflict and conflict resolution over time
- Changes in global systems over time

Component 5: The Study of Cross-Cultural Understanding/Interaction

Component 5 focuses on changing attitudes and behaviors. The elements of this component constitute the highest level of global cognition and compassion in that they require students to look beyond their own values and interests to a fuller comprehension and appreciation of those different than them. Merryfield (1995) identifies the elements of component 5 as follows:

- Understanding of one's own culture and heritage
- Understanding of multiple identities and loyalties
- Recognition of the complexity of cultural diversity and cultural universals
- The role of one's own culture in the world system
- Skills and experiences in seeing one's own culture from others' perspectives
- Experiences in learning about another culture and the world from another culture's values and worldviews
- Extended experiences with people significantly different from oneself
- Ability to communicate across cultures
- Ability to work with people from other cultures

Educational research shows that knowledge about problems alone is unlikely to lead to a change in values or appropriate action (Calder, 2000). If students are to act differently in the future and learn the knowledge, values, and skills necessary to build a better world for all, experiences with those whose culture differs from their own is necessary. Contact with another culture, however, does not necessarily create the cross-cultural acceptance desired and might actually reinforce stereotyping unless students have the knowledge to understand the reasons for differences in values and behaviors.

To support a change in attitude and behavior, Case (1993) identifies five key cognitive and affective attributes associated with developing a global perspective that global educators must address:

Open-mindedness: Case considers open-mindedness the crucial feature of developing perspective taking. It indicates willingness to base beliefs on the impartial consideration of available information.

Anticipation of complexity: Anticipation of complexity requires students to look beyond simplistic explanations of complex issues and to see the interrelationship of factors that created the issue. Therefore, Case stresses that educators must move away from presenting a definitive list of the causes of an event, to allow for a fuller understanding of all factors that contributed to a situation.

Resistance to stereotyping: Resistance to stereotyping refers to the ability to see beyond a narrow range of characteristics for individuals from a particular culture or nation. Case cautions that global educators may unintentionally promote stereotyping by allowing a quaint or exotic feature of a culture to become the focus of study.

Inclination to emphasize: An inclination to emphasize indicates a willingness to place oneself in the role or predicament of another or to imagine issues from another's perspective. The rationale for promoting empathy stems from the fact that merely learning about other people or countries might not increase students' understanding of that culture.

Nonchauvinism: Case defines nonchauvinism as the ability to avoid prejudging those with whom one is not affiliated and to accept the interests of others even if those interests are incompatible with one's own.

Anderson (1979) suggests that cross-cultural awareness begins when students realize that they are both *culture borrowers* and *culture depositors*. When students realize that their own culture is drawn from people from all geographic regions, they learn to accept and respect these cultures. It is equally important that they understand that parts of their culture are constantly integrated into the cultures of other nations. The emphasis in a global curriculum should focus more on the borrowing of ideas and the evolution of cultures than on the divisions among people or nations.

Component 6: Awareness of Human Choices

Component 6 expands on the previous five components with an emphasis on human choices. Students are reminded of the choices made in the past that have had a beneficial or an adverse effect on the world and are challenged to understand the long-range implications of their choices as global systems expand in the future. Calder (2000) stresses that students must acquire the skills, values, and attitudes that lead to a commitment for responsible choices that promotes the preservation and fair distribution of the earth's resources and builds a more just society, both locally and globally.

Component 7: Development of Analytical and Evaluative Skills

Merryfield (1975) includes the following elements in component 7:

* Abilities to collect, analyze, and evaluate information from different perspectives and worldviews
* Critical thinking skills
* Recognition of the role of values and worldview in inquiry

The elements of component 7 are not unique to global education. The goals of critical thinking, valuing diversity, and seeing connections are also essential to other disciplines and movements in education. However, these skills are critical if the goals of global education are to be met.

It is important that students develop skills in recognizing, analyzing, and evaluating the interconnections among local, regional, and global issues and between their personal lives and global events. They must search for alternative views, experiences, and methods that acknowledge equality of people within and between nations. A well-constructed global education program introduces students to the research process, including the information-gathering process that allows them to form testable propositions.

Component 8: Strategies for Participation and Involvement

In order to understand themselves and people different from themselves, students must have cross-cultural experiences in their own community, the nation, and the world. Skills in cross-cultural interaction and reflection, therefore, must be taught, learned, and practiced. Cross-cultural interaction allows students to demonstrate their ability to use cultural knowledge and skills in actual cross-cultural communication and conflict management. Component 8 addresses this need, and Merryfield (1995) includes the following elements:

* Cross-cultural interaction, participation, and collaboration
* Opportunities for making and implementing decisions
* Experiences with addressing real-life problems
* Attention to learning from experience

In a perfect world, all students would have the opportunity to travel and experience cultures different from their own. Obviously, the reality of education today makes this impossible. Whenever possible, students should be allowed to interact with those of other cultures. This interaction can occur through face-to-face meetings, guests in the classroom, correspondence, or multimedia events.

Merryfield (2003) feels that electronic cultural projects through the Internet provide the opportunity to increase cultural sensitivity and awareness for students as they develop skills and experiences needed in a global society. She notes that triggers of visual and aural differences often subconsciously make people uncomfortable or otherwise constrain people's ability to listen, interact, and learn from others in face-to-face interactions. Online interactions can reduce these triggers of differences and make students more comfortable asking questions they would never ask in a face-to-face interaction.

According to Merryfield (2003), it is unadvisable to provide a cross-cultural experience without first providing the substantive knowledge on which students can build perspective consciousness. Without an understanding of human beliefs and values, global systems, global issues and problems, and global history, such experiences may fail to meet the goals of cross-cultural understanding and acceptance and may actually reinforce the very prejudices and stereotypes a global curriculum is designed to end.

CONCLUSION

A review of the elements of global education makes one wonder why all educators do not embrace a global curriculum. Chapter 1 addressed many of those issues. The reluctance to provide a global curriculum, however, falls into two main categories.

Many educators who are reluctant to endorse global education programs feel the goals and objectives of curriculum materials and teacher-training programs are not clearly defined. Teachers may not feel competent to teach or administer programs in international issues, area studies, foreign languages, and cross-cultural understanding.

Budgetary limitations, inadequate preservice and in-service training for educators, and the limited availability of appropriate teaching resources and material all prevent the inclusion of global education in the curriculum.

The second reason is more philosophical in nature. Some educators are concerned that an emphasis on global or international programs is contradictory to the fundamental purpose of the school—to prepare young people for careers and for citizenship in the United States. They fear the result will be the demise of the influence of the United States in world affairs.

The values inherent in a global curriculum are core values for life in a democratic society. These include acceptance of and respect for others, open-mindedness, respect for human rights, concern for justice, commitment to democracy, and a willingness to be involved. These elements are necessary for the future of the United States and for the world. It is important that educators remember the words of Teilhard de Chardin when he stated that "the age of nations has passed. Now, unless we wish to perish we must shake off our old prejudices and build the earth."

INSTRUCTIONAL IDEAS

Teaching Human Rights

Many organizations provide excellent websites full of activities for teachers to use in their classrooms. One such organization is the United Nations. The global teaching and learning project at this site is called CyberSchoolBus. The site provides links to world resources, quizzes and games, community-building activities, information about current events, free teacher resources, and a global art gallery.

A curriculum resource titled Human Rights in Action is an interactive online activity where students find out what human rights are and then see what rights they themselves have and how they got those rights through activities, classroom discussions and question-and-answer sessions with experts.

Students plan an action to increase respect for human rights in their own communities and carry it out. They then send a brief report of their action to the UN CyberSchoolBus, and their report will become part of a global "atlas" of student actions on human rights.

Teaching Global Economics

Teaching economics to elementary and middle schoolers is sometimes a daunting task for educators. Appropriate instructional materials are difficult to find, but "Trading around the World" from the International Monetary Fund (IMF) provides just such a resource. Participants experience the challenges and excitement of international trade while playing this interactive, role-playing, educational game. Students see if they can get the best price for the goods they sell and the biggest bargains for the goods they buy. They must watch how the global economy is doing: the prices and the deals depend on how healthy the global economy is.

Also available from the IMF website is "Where in the World and What in the World Is Money?," an interactive world history of money. As students play this game, they discover that many different things have served as money throughout history and around the globe.

Teaching about Environmental Issues

What is the cultural significance of freshwater? The educators at the Center for Innovation in Engineering and Science Education in the Stevens Institute of Technology believe that students can learn much about other cultures by participating in online collaborative activities.

When participating in "Take a Dip: The Water in Our Lives," students team up with others around the globe to test freshwater. In this collaborative project, participants compare the water quality of their local river, stream, lake, or pond with other freshwater sources around the world.

The students assess the quality of water on the basis of physical characteristics and chemical substances; research and share anecdotes, stories, and practices dealing with water in local communities; identify and compare organisms in a water sample with other participating classes; and assess the quality of water based on macroscopic life found in the water. Then they look for relationships, trends, similarities, and differences among the data collected by all project participants.

Collaborative Online Projects

Looking for a collaborative project with a global focus? Look no further than Global Schoolhouse, a clearinghouse for collaborative projects from around the globe. These projects are hosted by the Global SchoolNet Foundation, other reputable organizations, and partner projects conducted by teachers worldwide.

An example of a past Global Schoolhouse project is "Face to Face," an international media education project in which secondary schools from all over Europe, the United States, and South Africa exchange video letters. The project encouraged international communication between young students from various ethnic groups. It promoted the intercultural and European dimension in schooling and the introduction of new media and innovative pedagogical practices. Teachers can also join Global Schoolhouse's Hilites, a mailing list that provides advance notice via e-mail of many excellent online projects from around the world.

INTERNET RESOURCES

Center for Innovation in Engineering and Science Education: http://k12science .ati.stevens-tech.edu/index.html
CyberSchoolBus: http://www.un.org/Pubs/CyberSchoolBus/index.html
Global Schoolhouse: http://www.gsn.org
Human Rights in Action: http://www.un.org/cyberschoolbus/humanrights/ index.asp
Take a Dip: The Water in Our Lives: http://k12science.ati.stevens-tech.edu/ curriculum/dipproj2/en/
Trading around the World: http://www.imf.org/external/np/exr/center/students/ trade/index.htm
United Nations: http://www.un.org
Where in the World and What in the World Is Money?: http://www.imf.org/ external/np/exr/center/students/money/index.htm

REFERENCES

Anderson, L. (1979). *Schooling and citizenship in a global age: An exploration of the meaning and significance of global education.* Bloomington, IN: Social Studies Development Center.

Calder, M. (2000). A concern for justice: Teaching using a global perspective in the classroom. *Theory into Practice, 39,* 81–87.

Case, R. (1993). Key elements of a global perspective. *Social Education, 57,* 318–323.

Gilliom, M. E. (1981). Global education and the social studies. *Theory into Practice, 20,* 169–173.

Hanvey, R. G. (1975). *An attainable global perspective.* New York: Center for War/Peace Studies.

Hendrix, J. C. (1998). Globalizing the curriculum. *Clearing House, 71,* 305–308.

Kniep, W. M. (1986). Defining a global education by its content. *Social Studies, 50,* 437–446.

McCabe, L. T. (1997). Global perspective development. *Education, 42,* 41–48.

Merryfield, M. M. (1991). Science-technology-society and global perspectives. *Theory into Practice, 30,* 287–293.

Merryfield, M. M. (1995). Institutionalizing cross-cultural experiences and international expertise in teacher education: The development and potential of a global education PDS network. *Journal of Teacher Education, 46,* 19–27.

Merryfield, M. M. (1997). A framework for teachers preparing teachers to teach global perspectives. In M. M. Merryfield, E. Jachow, & S. Pickert (Eds.), *Preparing teachers to teach global perspectives: A handbook for teacher educators.* Thousand Oaks, CA: Corwin Press.

Merryfield, M. M. (2001). Moving the center of global education: From imperial world views that divide the world to double consciousness, contrapuntal pedagogy, hybridity, and cross-cultural competence. In W. B. Stanley (Ed.), *Critical issues in social studies research for the 21st century.* Greenwich, CT: Information Age Publishing.

Merryfield, M. M. (2003). Like a veil: Cross-cultural experiential learning online. *Contemporary Issues in Technology and Teacher Education, 3,* 146–171.

Tye, B. B., & Tye, K. A. (1992). *Global education: A study of school change.* Albany: State University of New York Press.

CHAPTER 4

The Integration Model

The sun shines from the sky of azure blue. It can radiate peace all over the world. But peace can only prevail when we have learned that what is the same about each of us is more important than that which is different.

—Tibetan saying

In 1979, John Goodlad noted that most of the world's educational systems, including that of the United States, have as one of their goals developing understanding and appreciation of other nations, other cultures, and other people. Although most educators and politicians see the value of including global issues in the curriculum, the "how" of including global education in a crowded curriculum has been a topic of discussion for over twenty-five years.

This chapter describes an integrated approach to globalizing the curriculum. Global education should not be viewed as a matter of simply adding foreign language courses or a unit on international relations, nor should it be confined to social studies courses. Using an integrated approach, teachers incorporate global issues into the existing curriculum and find a place for global topics in all subject areas. Proponents of an integrated approach stress that providing a global perspective should not require the creation of new courses but rather should provide for the inclusion of global perspectives at every grade level and in every subject area.

If students are to develop a genuinely global outlook, they must come to recognize that virtually all aspects of their lives are influenced by developments beyond the United States. Global education, therefore, should not be viewed as the private domain or responsibility of any one teacher or any single subject area. Nor should it be equated with discrete subjects, such as history, foreign language, or geography. The subject matter of global education is found throughout the curriculum and can be drawn from all subject areas and can be studied in a variety of ways. Global education should be viewed as omnipresent, continuously woven throughout the student's entire school experience.

An integrated approach to global education is a logical choice for providing a global perspective because all global issues are cross disciplinary and include the arts, humanities, sciences, mathematics, foreign language, and social studies. Global education emphasizes an integration and infusion of content and process across the curriculum and throughout the school, designed to prepare students for responsible and informed world citizenship. At the core of global education is an imperative for addressing cultural diversity and improving cross-cultural understanding and competencies.

There are three primary methods of integrating global issues into the curriculum: infusion of the existing curriculum with global issues, parallel planning toward a common goal, and interdisciplinary/multidisciplinary planning by teachers from different disciplines. These methods often overlap and are used in a combination of ways. The first method, an infusion approach, is appropriate for individual teachers who wish to add a global perspective to their subject areas. The other two approaches, parallel planning and interdisciplinary planning, are designed for use by two or more faculty working together. Table 4.1 provides the basic elements of each of these three approaches.

Table 4.1   Strategies for an Integranted Approach to Global Education.

Strategy to be used by an individual teacher	Strategies to be used by the entire faculty or group of teachers	
Infusion Approach	Parallel Planning Approach	Interdisciplinary/Multidisciplinary Approach
Each area of a school's required curriculum or "hidden curriculum" is infused with global issues.	Two or more teachers plan together to meet a common goal and provide global issues and perspectives to the curriculum.	Teachers from different disciplines or subject areas plan to blend instruction or create instruction that enhances each other's instruction.

INFUSION OF GLOBAL ISSUES INTO THE CURRICULUM

Historically, curriculum has been viewed as the dividing of knowledge into distinct discipline or subject areas. Each area of a school's established curriculum, which includes these distinct areas of study, can be infused with global issues by teachers who take the time and effort to research ways of incorporating a global perspective into their daily lessons. In fact, Hendrix (1998) stresses that the infusion of global issues into the curriculum has been the most common approach to globalizing the curriculum for several reasons:

- Infusion broadens the responsibility among the faculty for helping students think about global issues in all disciplines. No longer is global education viewed as the responsibility of the social studies teacher.
- Separate courses in global education run the risk of having the topic viewed as something added to the curriculum rather than being a major focus of the curriculum.
- Infusion ensures that students are exposed to global issues in several contexts, providing for a greater understanding of the issues.
- Separate courses in global education may lead to the perception that global issues are a concern for a few teachers but not critical to the lives of most students.

If global education is to become an integral part of the curriculum in the near future, individual teachers must seize every opportunity to inject a global dimension into existing courses on a regular basis as well as seeking the introduction of new units and programs. The following are ways to infuse the curriculum:

- Teachers integrate references to their own travels and experiences to illustrate or explain something in the classroom.
- Music teachers incorporate music from all areas of the world into their lessons.
- Literature teachers choose poems and stories that represent the feelings and lives of individuals from every area of the world, making sure they include underrepresented groups.

- Social studies teachers begin each day with a review of the major current events from around the world and lead a discussion of how such events will affect their students.
- Science teachers discuss the impact of scientific developments in other parts of the world on the lives of their students.
- Physical education teachers teach games played in other parts of the world.
- Math teachers begin each day with a discussion of a famous mathematician, focusing on the concept of mathematics as a universal language.
- Sociology teachers teach about family structures, emphasizing the commonalities across cultures.

Infusing the curriculum with a global perspective requires additional planning and thought on the part of the teacher. The majority of the commercial materials focusing on global education, however, are intended to add a global perspective to ordinary curriculum topics and to fit into the regular curriculum. Such materials and learning activities allow integration, fit into a stream of classroom activities, promote focus and direction, and create richer learning environments. Global education materials should not be viewed as filler activities to be pulled out occasionally when time allows but rather as enrichment experiences that add to the depth of instruction.

The infusion of global issues can go beyond the established curriculum of a school and affect the "hidden curriculum" as well. Schools must be seen as total institutions since a student's preparation for global citizenship is affected by the informal as well as the formal curriculum. Schools, therefore, must be environments in which acceptance and appreciation exist for people from all backgrounds, regardless of cultural, gender, religious, or socioeconomic status. In these environments, students are taught that their actions and decisions affect others. In classrooms, students need to acquire a social sensitivity that allows them to look at realities from different viewpoints. Teachers provide a global perspective by teaching problem solving, peace education, and conflict resolution. Students who learn to resolve classroom conflict through peaceful means may see these same strategies as means to solve larger, more global issues.

The integration of global education into other subjects may be more complex than developing new courses in global studies. However, they emphasize that the opportunities for student learning will be greater than if single courses are developed and if the ideas in them are not related to other subject areas. The benefits of adding a global perspective for both students and teachers are both rewarding and insightful.

PARALLEL PLANNING FOR GLOBAL EDUCATION

Parallel planning describes the efforts of two or more teachers working toward common goals to add a global perspective. In this approach, an entire school or groups of faculty select a common theme and plan for instruction linked to the theme independently of one another. Anderson and Anderson (1979) describe the efforts of one school to bring a global orientation to students. The faculty of the school picked the following beliefs as overarching purposes for creating instruction:

- To develop students' understanding of themselves as individuals
- To develop students' understanding of themselves as members of the human species
- To develop students' understanding of themselves as inhabitants and dependents of the earth
- To develop students' understanding of themselves as participants in global society
- To develop within students the competencies required to live intelligently and responsibly as individuals, human beings, and members of global society

Levak, Merryfield, and Wilson (1993) describe the efforts of teachers at an Ohio high school to bring global connections into their curriculum. Their instructional goals focused around three major units: culture, conflict, and the interconnectedness between past civilizations and cultures today. As the central theme of the curriculum, culture provided a foundation for understanding people, issues, and systems. The instructors aimed to help students understand the complex nature of global issues (such as conflict) and global systems.

Using these common themes, teachers planned teaching strategies with the objective of incorporating global issues into the curriculum. Using the theme of culture, the teachers provided the following activities:

- The biology teacher had students identify ecosystems and classification systems as a way to define certain aspects of studying culture.
- The English teacher selected *Lord of the Flies* as required reading to help students understand how culture and governance develop and change over time.
- The social studies teacher selected concepts such as ethnocentrism and cultural diversity as subject matter.
- The math teacher used the analogy that bridges are needed across cultures, and students examined shapes and structures in the construction of famous world bridges.

The teachers brainstormed and selected concepts and teaching strategies from their own disciplines to complement the agreed-on theme. For parallel planning to be effective, however, each teacher must recognize the importance of the overall curriculum theme and the established goals. To coordinate the disciplines, this group of teachers found it helpful to develop a yearlong curriculum map in order to prevent the overlapping of content while still complementing each other's instruction.

INTERDISCIPLINARY/MULTIDISCIPLINARY APPROACH TO GLOBAL EDUCATION

The interdisciplinary/multidisciplinary approach weaves two or more disciplines together in the presentation of global issues. Unlike parallel planning, this approach requires teachers from different disciplines or subject areas to blend or to create instruction that enhances the others' teaching strategies. The interdisciplinary/multidisciplinary approach seems most appropriate since the very nature of global education is interdisciplinary. The fundamental ideas in global education—global interdependence, contending worldviews, multicultural understanding, and global perspectives—emphasize the interdisciplinary connections that are broader in scope than those fundamental ideas within a specific discipline.

Merryfield (1997) suggests that an interdisciplinary/multidisciplinary approach is appealing to teachers who are looking for holistic approaches to global education that might bridge several disciplines. These teachers realize that no single area of study is broad enough to be the only basis for global education. Merryfield argues that such key issues as food, energy, pollution, defense and security, resource use, and human rights require an approach that goes beyond the instruction that can be offered in a single discipline.

Although the use of an interdisciplinary/multidisciplinary approach is pedagogically sound, interdisciplinary concepts are abstract, and teaching them is often difficult. In emphasizing interdisciplinary concepts, global educators help students apply what they have learned from one context to other situations. Through interdisciplinary instruction, students' engagement is heightened, and they retain more information since the information is presented in a variety of learner modalities. Cooperative learning, simulation, student projects, and community service may be successful pedagogical strategies and techniques that make global connections more interesting, more effective, and easier to obtain. Interdisciplinary strategies allow teachers to draw on their students' experiences and organize their instruction through intermediary strategies that lead to better comprehension and understanding.

Interdisciplinary/multidisciplinary approaches abound. Expansion and improvement of the study of world history, world geography, world economics, and world ecology occurs when teachers plan strategies with other teachers to help bring these subjects alive for students. Social studies teachers often work with language arts teachers to select novels, poems, and essays to emphasize the topics being taught. Others seek to expand students' understanding of cultural diversity though the cross-cultural study of literature, art, music, dance, religion, and social customs. The following three methods for providing an interdisciplinary/multicultural emphasis to global education are the most common:

1. Teachers of core subjects (social studies, language arts, science, and mathematics) work together to present an interdisciplinary focus to the topic. Language arts teachers help students prepare essays on topics learned in science or social studies. Mathematics

teachers focus on math concepts that further the comprehension of topics presented in social studies or science.

2. Teachers of related arts (physical education, art, music, and drama) work with core teachers or with teachers in the elementary grades to present an interdisciplinary focus to the topic. When studying a particular country or region, the physical education teachers present games typically played in that region. The art teacher may have students create murals to depict the students' understanding of a concept taught in a core class. The music teacher specifically selects pieces that represent a region or country studied.

3. Teachers from all areas of the school plan and work together to present information about a global issue. They may plan of activities revolving around Earth Day or United Nations Day with the idea that all activities in the school will be centered on this one theme.

Planning multidisciplinary lessons can be challenging because an interdisciplinary curriculum is dynamic and ever evolving. A global approach to instruction calls for an increased breadth of knowledge for teachers, as they are asked to expand instruction beyond their subject area and to learn new content. Teachers also require general global knowledge as well as information specific to the subjects they teach.

In their work with teachers using an interdisciplinary approach, Levak et al. (1993) found that a curriculum map and guiding themes are critical elements of a successful interdisciplinary program. The success of such a program depends primarily on the teachers' willingness to actively participate. Teachers who work together to teach global issues through an interdisciplinary approach are often invigorated by looking at material outside their content area, learning to be generalists, and practicing the skills in cooperative learning that they teach their students.

CONCLUSION

If global education is viewed as simply another content area competing with traditional subjects for space in an already overcrowded curriculum, it is doomed to have little impact. Likewise, if global education instruction is limited to isolated bits of time and energy in the form of such activities as "global education week" or "foreign culture day," the effect on students will probably be minimal. Therefore, the use of an integrated approach to global education ensures that global education is a prominent part of the curriculum that accomplishes the following:

- Leads to connections that will increase in intensity with time and events
- Helps students understand the ramifications of culture and that people may interpret an event or issue in different ways
- Spans time and space
- Helps students perceive the qualities of humanness they share with different cultures
- Helps students see the commonality within diversity

When John Goodlad applauded the inclusion of global issues in the curriculum several decades ago, he warned that the inclusion of information about other nations, other cultures, and other people must not lead to a "we-they" way of thinking. A global education program that integrates the contributions, concerns, and needs of people across the world creates an environment in which such a way of thinking is eliminated and in which recognition and acceptance of the world's people becomes a lifetime process.

INSTRUCTIONAL IDEAS

Integrated Activities

Global learning activities frequently address more than one subject area. Students are required to apply their knowledge from several disciplines to complete the task. The objectives of the Global Sun Temperature Project from CIESE address primarily math and science standards. At the completion of the project, however, students will have practiced skills and learned new information involving not only math and science but also technology, geography, reading, and writing.

While participating in this project, students determine their latitude and longitude coordinates, measure and record temperature and minutes of daylight, calculate averages, plot and analyze data, draw conclusions based on raw data from the Internet, and communicate their results. Students also have the opportunity to interact with other students from around the world and study their geographic location, environment, and culture.

Seven specific lesson plans to use in conjunction with this project are available at the website. Four of the lesson plans target math and science skills, two address language arts standards, and one focuses on geography skills.

Peace Education

What kind of activities can be used to teach about world peace? PeaceQuest is a WebQuest designed to engage society in a dialogue to eliminate hatred and bigotry, to foster understanding and tolerance, and to bring peace to our world.

To accomplish this goal, groups of students use a variety of websites to create a video talk show or documentary; create a Web page, multimedia presentation, newsletter, or public awareness brochure; write a letter to the editor that they will send to newspapers online with their answer to the question, "How can we make our world safe for children?"; or create a PeaceQuest Poster to display on the school website.

Several useful features are included in this Web-based lesson. Process guides are available to guide students as they brainstorm and create interview questions for the project. Rubrics for each of the tasks are an integral component of this WebQuest, ensuring that students clearly understand project requirements.

Multicultural Appreciation

"What if a child in Los Angeles, who views sports figures and celebrities as heroes, could get to know a Tibetan child whose main goal in life is to develop the level of compassion attained by the Tibetan Lamas? What would happen if children from fundamentally different backgrounds were enabled to build relationships with each other and work in partnership to solve problems together?" The goals of the BRIDGES to Understanding online classroom program are to provide a culturally sensitive curriculum that encourages exploration and exchange between cultures and to inspire other educators to build their own BRIDGES.

Developed by photographer Phil Borges, BRIDGES is a cross-cultural collaboration that connects students worldwide through digital storytelling. This project connects students from indigenous cultures with those in more urban surroundings. The students in participating schools create interactive photographic stories while being mentored by a number of professionals.

The project defines culture as "the root from which we grow. It gives us strength, our definition, our uniqueness, our way of life." This telecomputing project leads students to a deeper understanding of their own culture and the culture of others as well as an understanding of how cultural customs and beliefs affect the environment.

Inspiring Activism

Global education provides a solid foundation for students to understand their world, but how can they be actively involved in making a difference? TakingITGlobal (TIG) is an international organization led by youths and powered by technology. TIG brings young people together with international networks to collaborate on projects addressing global problems and creating positive change.

The sixteen-page *Guide to Action* is a downloadable document that guides students through the steps of identifying opportunities for action, developing projects, and posting their projects on the TIG website. TIG members from around the world can join projects posted at the site. Over 53,000 members from 241 countries participate in the almost 900 projects available.

One example is Act 4 Peace, a project developed by students in the United Kingdom. The goal of the project is to find young actors, writers, or musicians interested in educating young people in schools about the importance of unity, tolerance, and peace in the world today. More than thirty participants from around the world have joined this project to provide and create music and drama materials and resources that can be used to draw attention to injustices throughout the world.

INTERNET RESOURCES

Act 4 Peace: http://projects.takingitglobal.org/act4peace
BRIDGES: http://www.bridgesweb.org/
Global Sun Temperature Project: http://k12science.ati.stevens-tech.edu/
curriculum/tempproj3/en/index.shtml
PeaceQuest: http://www.lausd.k12.ca.us/lausd/offices/di/Burleson/Lessons/
PeaceQuest/index.htm
TakingITGlobal: http://www.takingitglobal.org/

REFERENCES

Anderson, L., & Anderson, C. (1979). A visit to Middleton's world-centered
school: A scenario. In J. M. Becker (Ed.), *Schooling for a global age.* New
York: McGraw-Hill.

Goodlad, J. I. (1979). Foreword. In J. M. Becker (Ed.), *Schooling for a global
age.* New York: McGraw-Hill.

Hendrix, J. C. (1998). Globalizing the curriculum. *Clearing House, 71,*
305–308.

Levak, B., Merryfield, M., & Wilson, R. (1993). Global connections. *Educational Leadership, 51,* 73–75.

Merryfield, M. M. (1997). A framework for teachers preparing teachers to
teach global perspectives. In M. M. Merryfield, E. Jachow, & S. Pickert
(Eds.), *Preparing teachers to teach global perspectives: A handbook for
teacher educators* (pp. 1–25). Thousand Oaks, CA: Corwin Press.

CHAPTER 5

The Unit Approach

Look closely at the present you are constructing. It should look like
the future you dream of.

—Alice Walker, Witness for Peace lectionary archives
(http://www.witnessforpeace.org/)

When most teachers recall how they were taught global issues, they remember units of study in social studies classes that focused on a particular country. The cumulating activity of these units was often an opportunity to sample food from that country or to hear a presentation
from someone who had lived in or visited the country being studied.
Units focusing on particular countries or cultures have been a mainstay
of global education, and this chapter presents the strategies for providing global education through this traditional unit format.

Global education is often content bound when teachers use thematic
units of instruction that focus on the study of foreign and international issues. These units can last from a few days to several weeks with the goal
of systematically integrating relationships, patterns, and abstractions that
join different aspects of our world together. The common example of the
instructional unit is a set of lessons that focuses on another culture, country, or geographic region of the world. Units are often taught in government or civics classes, presenting studies of foreign policy, international
relations, or world problems. Units are used in science classes to deal
with the universal issues involving global systems. Teachers of humanities classes often create units focusing on the contributions of books, music, and art from a certain region or nation. These curriculum-based units

often revolve around the key concepts of interdependence, cultural perspective, peace development, and conflict resolution.

ISSUES WITH THE TRADITIONAL UNIT APPROACH

Unfortunately, units often are developed in such a way that they become simply a superficial introduction to a number of countries, cultures, and customs. As a way of introducing students to a particular country or culture, teachers turn to what Begler (1998) calls the "five Fs":

Fashion: What people of a particular culture wear (or in some cases what they don't wear) becomes a focus of discussion. Students are presented cultural traditions involving clothing for the country studied.

Fiestas: Study involves traditional holidays and celebrations of this country. How and why these events are celebrated is discussed. Included is a discussion of the games children play and what they do for fun.

Folklore: Every country has legends, folklore, and myths. The stories handed down through generations become the focus of this discussion.

Famous people: The real and fictitious people who are primary to this country make up the focus of this discussion. Included are the accomplishments of these people. Inventors, heroes, writers, artists, politicians, and others who have had an impact on the country and the world are studied.

Food: Because the sharing and preparing of food is such a major event in every person's life, a discussion of food is necessary. Often, the emphasis is on the exotic food items people of a particular culture eat that make them different. A discussion of the mainstay diets is included. A typical conclusion of a unit on a particular country includes an opportunity to sample native dishes.

By focusing only on the things that make the country different and unique, however, students sometimes become "cultural tourists." This concept is based on the idea that each culture is a mosaic of places, traditions, art forms, celebrations, and experiences that portray a nation or people, and it is these characteristics that reflect the diversity and character of the country.

This method of providing globalization to the classroom also is known as the foods–costumes–customs approach. Too often, the content presented is limited to relatively superficial features and does little to create the global experiences desired for students. Textbooks and the traditional curriculum tend to reinforce stereotypes rather than tackle current events and challenge existing perspectives. This shallow exposure to unusual ethnic dishes and diverse holiday practices is unlikely to promote an enlightened perspective on the lives and concerns of people from other cultures. By attending to limited and somewhat trivial cultural dimensions, teachers may actually reinforce stereotypical perceptions rather than eliminate them. It is not enough, for example, to teach students that a main food source in Asian countries is rice. It is more important that they come to an understanding of why rice is a major food source. Merely having more information may not advance students' understanding, and simply teaching more about the world is not the solution for effective global education.

It is more important that students come to understand that all people have developed a material culture—housing, foods, dress, tools, and art—that fits their needs and environment. Cultures develop unique forms of work, play, and aesthetic expression in addition to languages and other systems of communication. They have advanced social organizations that provide the means for social control as well as the transmission of social values. Cultures also have formal and informal systems for education, rituals for expressing their worldviews and beliefs, and mechanisms and organizations for carrying out various economic functions. Therefore, our goals should be that students learn to appreciate the commonality within the diversity of a culture and understand the qualities of humanness that they share with those who are different from themselves.

Fleming (1991), however, suggests that there is a place for the five Fs in global education. At the K–3 level, a global perspective can be created by exposure to these elements and by having students explore how families live throughout the world. This, of course, includes studying about a society's clothes, food, holidays, and customs. At these younger grade levels, the curriculum gives attention to ethnic and cultural diversity while still focusing on developing a sense of local community because it is with their own local community that these students have a personal connection. If students are allowed to explore these elements within their own community and come to understand why they themselves dress, eat, and celebrate the way they do, they will be more accepting of those in other communities and begin to adopt a more global perspective.

Students are thought to be studying global education when they are learning about another culture, country, or geographic region of the world or when they are studying foreign policy or international relations. Many educators think of global education as a content-bounded domain, involving only the study of things foreign or international. The trouble with this concept is not that it is wrong; it is simply a narrow and incomplete notion of global education.

Global education often begins with teaching about the local community. When students can make the connection between the issues and concerns of their neighbors and then the larger world beyond, they are as much involved in global education as they are when studying communities in another part of the world. If the material is presented correctly and with a focus on the concepts important to all humans, students can be involved in global education, whether studying their own communities or studying communities in other parts of world. A study of the American Revolution in a U.S. history class, for example, can involve students in the investigation of global issues as much as when they study the Arab–Israeli conflict in an international relations course.

According to Merryfield (2002), global educators must resist the simplification of other cultures and confront stereotypes and exotica. For example, if, in an introduction to a unit on the Middle East, a teacher tries to motivate students by presenting exotic images—such as harems, polygamy, belly dancing, sheiks, and camel races—the teacher will actually reinforce the very stereotypes global education seeks to eliminate. If the teacher fails to challenge students' stereotypes that all people from the Middle East are supporters of terrorism or that all Muslim women have few rights, students will have difficulty developing a global perspective. Teachers must focus on developing lessons that replace misinformation with opportunities for understanding the complexity of cultures, cultural conflicts, and global issues.

STRATEGIES FOR THE EFFECTIVE USE OF THE UNIT APPROACH

The unit as an instructional method does have a place in global education, as it provides what Case (1993) identifies as the two dimensions of globalizing the curriculum: substantive and perceptual. The substantive dimension is a working understanding of the various aspects of the world and how they function together. These things are often learned in content-specific courses and provide a foundation on which students can build a more abstract global perceptual understanding. The second dimension, the perceptual, is more advanced and "involves nurturing perspectives that are empathic, free of stereotypes, not predicated on naive or simplistic assumptions, and not colored by prejudicial statements" (p. 318).

If developed correctly, units that focus on a country explore science issues that are global or demonstrate the contributions of international artists and musicians can provide both substantive and perceptual dimensions. Units can provide a foundation on which students make personal connections with those who live in other countries. This can lead to an understanding that all humans have the same hopes and desires for the future. Table 5.1 provides a summary of the effective strategies for the use of the unit approach to global education.

Pike (2000) notes that units that develop a global perspective provide several broad concepts: interdependence, connectedness, global perspectives, and multiple perspectives. Interdependence occurs when students begin to understand the connections they have with people and environments in other parts of the world. It comes with the realization that our society could not exist as it does without the contributions of those in other parts of the world.

Connectedness develops when students see the link between areas of knowledge, curriculum subjects, aspects of schooling, and humans and their environments. Connectedness occurs when students combine the substantive and perceptual dimensions to form a more complete understanding of global issues. These two elements are achieved when students understand that they are responsible members of the global community.

Table 5.1   Strategies for the Effective Use of the Traditional Unit Format.

- Presentations must avoid superficial and exotic descriptions.
- Goals should revolve around the key concepts of interdependence, cultural perspective, peace development, and conflict resolution.
- Activities of unit should focus on presentation of content knowledge, exposure to diverse cultures and experiences, and opportunities for authentic application.
- Instructional strategies should include debates, student research, student presentations, service projects, and cooperative learning.

Perspective is also critical and describes two types of perspectives that are the focus of global education. The first, a global perspective, is generally interpreted to mean the provision of insights, ideas, and information that enable students to look beyond the confines of local and national boundaries in their thinking and aspirations. The second, multiple perspectives, is the ability to consider differing views on any issue before reaching a judgment.

Bacon and Kischner (2002) suggest that an understanding of different perspectives provides a crucial framework on which to build a global curriculum. Helping students develop a knowledge and skill base that has relevance to understanding and engaging in such a complex world requires three elements: content knowledge, exposure to diverse cultures and experiences, and authentic application. Therefore, units designed to provide a global perspective should address these three elements.

The first element, content knowledge, is critical for the development of a global perspective. It is content knowledge that lays the foundation for the development of the substantive dimension of global education. Historical knowledge, which includes the evolution of universal and diverse human values, the development of our contemporary global systems, and the causes of today's global issues and problems, is fundamental to global education. This historical background must be accurate and bias free.

Content knowledge can be developed by examining different points of view on a historical event, controversial issues, or current events. Through research on these topics and classroom discussions and presentations, students develop the habit of looking for and considering other perspectives, especially those of people from minority cultures or from other continents who are rarely the focus of textbooks, newspapers, or the media.

This look at underrepresented groups is critical for U.S. students who have a tendency to be unaware of the contributions and perspectives of other races, nations, and cultures. That lack of awareness arises partly because U.S. educators often emphasize experiences from a North American or European perspective when presenting international issues in science, music, and art. This is partly a reflection of their own educational experiences and partly a result of the lack of emphasis on underrepresented groups in the textbooks they select.

The second element in Bacon and Kischner's (2002) framework is exposure to diverse cultures and experiences. Interdependence and connectedness occur only when students have an opportunity to interact on a one-to-one basis with real people whose lives and cultures are different from their own. Such exposure includes classroom presentations by immigrants and visitors to the United States with inspiring experiences to share. International students from local universities or exchange students from other parts of the world may come to share life experiences and cultural information with the students of all ages. E-mail pen pals and videoconferencing exchanges with students in other countries also provide opportunities for cultural experiences with other people from around the world.

Merryfield (2002) found that such interaction must be long-term, ongoing activities rather than merely superficial experiences that do not allow participants sufficient time to build relationships. Having only one e-mail encounter or one international visit may actually reinforce existing stereotypes. Having someone come for one day and describe the elements of the five Fs will do little to eliminate false impressions and perceptions. However, if students have an opportunity to learn that they share the same concerns, desires, and emotions as those from other parts of the world, global understanding and acceptance will occur.

Obviously, a valuable way to develop a global perspective would be by traveling to another country and becoming familiar with that culture and getting to know those people. Although it is highly unlikely that teachers will have the resources to take their classes on field trips to other countries, teachers can take advantage of opportunities for personal travel abroad. This personal exposure to different cultures is invaluable for exploring other ways of life and collecting teaching materials to use in the classroom. These experiences lead to a depth and quality of teacher understanding and make the teaching of international topics and issues a natural way of presenting material.

The final element suggested by Bacon and Kischner (2002) is the authentic application of the elements presented in a global education program. Probably the best example of authentic application can be found in foreign language classes where students are required to demonstrate on a daily basis their comprehension by actually using the language. Often students in foreign language classes are given opportunities for investigating the various cultures of the countries where the language is spoken. While foreign language classes provide valuable experiences for the authentic application of a global perspective, it is more difficult to see other examples in schools because actual exposure to other cultures is limited in most settings.

Participating in debates concerning global issues is an effective way for students to develop multiple perspectives as they are forced to consider various sides of an issue. Debates can occur in almost any subject and might include a debate regarding the Israeli–Palestinian conflict in social studies, the building of pipelines in endangered ecosystems in science, and the merits of the contributions of writers in language arts. Teenagers care about injustice, and debates provide them an opportunity to explore these topics in depth. Through exploring the global picture of human rights violations, students become aware of and develop a desire to act on that awareness.

Participation in service projects is a valuable way to actively involve students in global issues. Many schools involve their students in book drives, toy drives, and the collection of money to address global needs. These projects need not be international in nature for students to understand the needs of others. Service to groups such as Habitat for Humanity provides excellent opportunities for young people to develop a more global perspective. Participants in this type activity often increase their empathy for those who are struggling; however, it is important that participation in a service project does not create a sense of superiority that leads to biases and patronizing attitudes toward other people. Students should understand that at some point all societies struggle and have needs, and it is the role of the fellow citizens of the world to reach out in these times of need.

Cooperative learning activities should be a cornerstone of the teaching strategies within a unit because cooperative learning advances the goals of global education. In a cooperative learning situation, students learn to accept the strengths and weaknesses of others, develop interpersonal skills, and resolve conflict. Within cooperative activities, individuals seek outcomes that are beneficial to themselves and beneficial to all other group members. Cooperative learning situations naturally produce a positive interdependence among students' goal attainments; students perceive that they can reach their learning goals if—and only if—the other students in the learning group reach their goals as well. As students develop these cooperative skills in their classrooms, they can better relate to the application of similar skills in global issues.

CONCLUSION

Schools are simply smaller versions of the broader world that exists beyond the school walls. Teachers must model the hopes and dreams they have for the future in their daily interactions with students, colleagues, and the community. They must demonstrate the level of involvement and curiosity they hope to inspire in their students. Educators must teach in such a way that the goals for a global society and better world can be met. Any model of global education—the global curriculum, the integration approach, or the traditional unit—must put understanding perspectives and authentic application at its core.

Teachers must reach out to the resources available in the local community as well as global resources available through technology to help students appreciate and accept those who are different from themselves. "Classrooms are greatly enriched when they are defined not by the four walls that enclose them, but as a nexus of community resources that teachers can draw on to build understanding of the greater world" (Bacon and Kischner, 2002, p. 51).

INSTRUCTIONAL IDEAS

Understanding Other Cultures

Multimedia presentations are effective tools for students to exhibit their knowledge by creating products they can share with others. Websites, videos, or slide presentations all allow students to imaginatively demonstrate what they have learned.

Developing presentations based on investigations of other cultures helps students synthesize new information. Rather than concluding a unit with a report or paper, a multimedia presentation assignment allows students to combine pictures, music, video, and text to construct a unique product.

A clearly defined project assignment provides the necessary structure for the students as they create their presentation. One assignment idea is an ABCs project. After investigating various resources for information about a particular culture, the students identify an interesting fact for each letter of the alphabet and create a website or slide show illustrating the information.

An example of this instructional idea can be seen at Discovering China with the ABCs, where third graders have researched Chinese culture, written descriptions of topics of interest, illustrated the topics, and published their work on a website.

Finding Information

The Internet has truly made the world a smaller place, particularly when it comes to finding information. Several excellent resources are available that enable students and teachers to access, compare, and analyze vast amounts of data relating to all the countries of the world.

The CIA World Factbook provides national-level information on countries, territories, and dependencies. This website provides detailed information about the geography, people, government, economy, communications, transportation, military, and transnational affairs of every country.

CountryReports profiles more than 260 countries on more than 6,600 pages. In addition to data similar to that found in the CIA World Factbook, CountryReports includes the history, the flag, the national anthem, information about the weather, and a reference map for each country.

A component of the United Nations CyberSchoolBus, the Country @ a Glance website features an interactive map, helping students visualize locations of the world with reference to each other. A click on a country reveals a few facts, such as population, area, and currency. While this site does not contain as much information as the other two, it may be appropriate for younger students.

Interactive Geography

Geonet is an interactive geography game for upper elementary students from the Kids' Place at Houghton Mifflin. Students may choose to play the World Game at one of two difficulty levels. Each level contains six categories that address the six major concepts of social studies: the world in spatial terms, places and regions, physical systems, human systems, environment and society, and the uses of geography.

Players can answer up to five questions from each category and then proceed to a different category. As students play the came, they accumulate points to become a GeoAdvisor, a GeoExpert, and a GeoChampion. This colorful animated site is kid friendly, is easy to navigate, and can be used by students individually or in groups.

Communicating Internationally

Teaching.com is a website that provides several excellent resources to enable international communication and develop a global focus in the classroom. The first is KeyPals Club, a place for young people, teachers, and students to locate and correspond with other youths and students around the world. The service provides an easy-to-use interface and database to quickly locate and contact a student or a class from around the world. Teachers can start a project with another class or create a new friendship with someone on the other side of the globe. Registration is quick and easy, and teachers and students have an effective method of global communication.

Intercultural E-Mail Classroom Connections (IECC) is another global communications tool from Teaching.com. Created in 1992 by three professors from St. Olaf College in Minnesota, IECC was one of the first services on the Web to facilitate international pen-pal exchanges between teachers and classrooms around the globe. At the IECC site, teachers in primary and secondary schools and higher education seek partner classrooms, teachers and volunteers age fifty and older seek intergenerational exchanges, participants discuss issues related to the use of e-mail in intercultural classroom connections, and teachers and students gather information from a global audience.

INTERNET RESOURCES

CIA World Factbook: http://www.odci.gov/cia/publications/factbook/index.html

CountryReports: http://www.countryreports.org/

CyberSchoolBus: http://www.un.org/Pubs/CyberSchoolBus/
Discovering China with the ABCs: http://www.fi.edu/fellows/fellow1/apr99/
   abc/index.html
Teaching.com: http://www.teaching.com/

REFERENCES

Bacon, N. A., & Kischner, G. A. (2002). Shaping global classroom. *Educational Leadership*, *60*, 48–51.

Begler, E. (1998). Global cultures—The first steps toward understanding. *Social Education*, *62*, 272–275.

Case, R. (1993). Key elements of a global perspective. *Social Education*, *57*, 318–323.

Fleming, D. B. (1991). Social studies reform and global education. *Social Studies*, *82*, 11–16.

Merryfield, M. M. (2002). The difference a global educator can make. *Educational Leadership*, *60*, 18–21.

Pike, G. (2000). Global education and national identity: In pursuit of meaning. *Theory into Practice*, *39*, 64–73.

Part 3

STRATEGIES FOR GLOBALIZING
THE CURRICULUM

The previous chapters featured overviews of the philosophical considerations, key concepts, and theories that are involved in a curriculum targeted toward global education. Rationales for promoting a global perspective in schools, fundamental issues, and requirements for determining priorities were the focus. In the following section, the educational processes dealing with methodologies and pedagogy are examined and discussed.

A global curriculum should be infused in all subject areas. It requires providing a global perspective for all curriculum areas at all levels, including literature, the arts, the sciences, and the extracurricular experiences of students. The remaining chapters of this book provide strategies and methods for globalizing the curriculum with particular focus on the teaching of social studies, science, health and physical education, literature, and mathematics.

CHAPTER 6

Global Education and Social Studies

The earth is but one country and mankind its citizens.

—Bahá'u'lláh, prophet and founder of the Bahá'í faith (1988).
Gleanings from the Writings of Bahá'u'lláh by Bahá'u'lláh,
translated by Shoghi Effendi. Wilmette: Bahá'í Publishing Trust

The cornerstone of many global initiatives can be found in the social studies classroom. Social studies content deals with places and cultures, therefore encompassing a curriculum that lends itself to a discussion of global issues and concerns. Teachers of social studies have been the leading advocates for the inclusion of global issues into the curriculum, although not all social studies teachers support this movement. In 1982, the National Council for the Social Studies (NCSS) issued a position statement on the need for global education. This statement provided two important reasons for the inclusion of global issues into the social studies curriculum:

1. The growing interrelatedness of life on our planet has increased the need for citizens to possess the knowledge and sensitivity required to comprehend the global dimensions of political, economic, and cultural phenomena.
2. Our nation's security, prosperity, and way of life are dependent in large part on citizens developing the capacity to comprehend transnational, cross-cultural interactions and to participate constructively in decisions influencing foreign policy (p. 36).

More recently, the need for global education was reemphasized in a position paper published by the NCSS (2001) that states,

> NCSS believes that an effective social studies program must include global and international education. Global and international education are important because the day-to-day lives of average citizens around the world are influenced by burgeoning international connections. The human experience is an increasingly globalized phenomenon in which people are constantly being influenced by transnational, cross-cultural, multi-cultural and multi-ethnic interactions. The goods we buy, the work we do, the cross-cultural links we have in our own communities and outside them, and increased worldwide communication capabilities all contribute to an imperative that responsible citizens understand global and international issues. The increasing globalization in the human condition has created additional opportunities and responsibilities for individuals and groups to take personal, social, and political action in the international arena.

In the twenty years between these two position statements, the need for a global focus in the social studies curriculum has increased exponentially. It is now apparent that the focus on global issues and concerns is not only desired but also needed at every grade level. The NCSS (1994) recommends that in the early grades, students should examine global connections and develop an understanding of the basic issues, concerns, and struggles of a global society. Middle school students should analyze interactions among states and nations as well as the cultural complexities that are developed by global events and change. High school students should begin to think systematically about personal, national, and global decisions at the same time as addressing critical issues such as peace, human rights, trade, and global ecology.

THE ROLE OF THE SOCIAL STUDIES TEACHER IN PROVIDING A GLOBAL CURRICULUM

Because of their academic and professional training along with the nature of the subjects they teach, social studies teachers are in a key position to assume a leading role in bringing a global perspective to the classroom. It is the social studies teacher who provides a range of global perspectives in the various content areas that prepare students to work and live in the twenty-first century. It is the responsibility of the social studies teacher to develop and implement strategies for the establishment of global perspectives that will affect the students not only in the classroom but also throughout the entire school and community.

However, many social studies teachers hesitate to provide a global focus to their curriculum. Some are conflicted because they see their primary role as being that of promoting the basic concepts and values that underlie America's democratic and constitutional order. Addressing a global perspective in the teaching of social studies has presented a challenge to these teachers who see their role as that of instilling the ideas of democracy and national pride. They struggle when asked to teach ethnic, cultural, socioeconomic ideas that might conflict with those of American society. Although some may believe that studying other cultures is worthwhile, they are hesitant to provide a picture of the United States as anything but the dominant culture of the world.

A second, more pragmatic reason for hesitation in including global issues and concerns in the curriculum is the lack of available resources and training. Many teachers feel there are inadequate resources to provide the type of focus they desire, and they find few resources written from a non-U.S. point of view; however, today's technology can serve as both a teaching tool and an educational resource. There is a wealth of quality information available online to make instruction in global issues effective and stimulating.

Social studies teachers must now see their role as that of preparing students to be productive world citizens. To do this, teachers must, as Gilliom (1981) states, "serve as living examples of the globally concerned citizen they are attempting to produce" (p. 171). Therefore, as teachers prepare to provide a global curriculum to their students, they must do the following:

- Consider their own attitudes and expectations of the global learning environment
- Have sufficient materials and useful content
- Use instructional strategies and techniques that ensure unprejudiced pedagogy
- Have adequate professional education and training on global issues

- Be convinced of the need to add a global dimension to their teaching
- Keep abreast of international matters
- Possess a global perspective and sensitivity to the challenges and promises that are a part of the living in a complex, interdependent world

NATIONAL CURRICULUM STANDARDS FOR SOCIAL STUDIES

As a first step in preparing a global focus for the social studies classroom, national standards should be considered. A task force of the NCSS developed the National Curriculum Standards for Social Studies in 1994. These standards include ten broad thematic strands, one of which, Standard IX, has as its emphasis global connections. All ten standards, however, provide teachers with an opportunity to help students develop an understanding of cultural differences and similarities as well as a realization of global interdependence. The ten national standards of the NCSS follow.

Culture

Social studies programs should include experiences that provide for the study of culture and cultural diversity.

Human beings create, learn, and adapt culture. Culture helps us understand ourselves both as individuals and as members of various groups. Human cultures exhibit similarities and differences, and they have unique systems of beliefs, knowledge, values, and traditions. In a multicultural society, students need to appreciate multiple perspectives that derive from different cultural vantage points. This understanding will allow them to relate to people in their own communities and throughout the world.

The essence of understanding global issues is the understanding of the concept of *culture*. Unfortunately, the misinterpretations and undervaluing of those cultures different from our own sometimes lead to teaching that alienates rather than unifies. This appears to be especially true of schools and students in the United States. Americans have been accused of cultural myopia because they use the culture of the United States as the measuring stick for all other cultures (Gilliom, 1981). Global education must address common social, political, economic, health, and environmental issues that affect all people. Therefore, when attempting to include cultural issues in the curriculum, educators need to be aware that shallow and stereotypical approaches marginalize different cultures and trivialize ethnic and cultural values. Table 6.1 provides examples of approaches for teaching in regard to different cultures that should be avoided.

Table 6.1   Approaches to Avoid When Teaching about Other Cultures.

They are different approach
This approach looks only at those things that are different from one's own culture. The emphasis is on what is different, not on those things that are similar. This approach reinforces cultural stereotypes.

They need us approach
This approach focuses on how much people from this culture need the assistance of the United States. If people in this culture provide services and goods to the United States, this is viewed as an arrangement that satisfies people on both sides. Our dependence on this culture is never acknowledged.

They are desperate approach
This approach shows another country as absolutely desperate, with its citizens dying of starvation, floods, hurricanes, and earthquakes. The citizens of the United States are viewed as saviors and rescuers.

They deserve what they get approach
This approach suggests that poverty, war, and genocide are something that happens to those who are less privileged or who are deserving of these tragedies. The causes of problems are not identified. The connections to the issues of prejudice and power are not presented.

They haven't progressed approach
This approach uses a "caught in time" concept. The films and books used to describe this country are outdated and show life as it was twenty or thirty years ago. The focus is on a critical period of history rather than the advances and events since this event. For example, Japan is shown as it was during the World War II rather than the thriving country it is today.

They are exotic, bizarre, or primitive approach
This approach focuses only on those customs or rituals that students will find exotic or bizarre. In order to create interests, teachers focus on the "weird" or "strange." The reasons for these customs or rituals are not shared, so students never come to understand why they occur.

Two websites provide useful information when teaching about various cultures. Exworthy Educational Resources provides information and teaching materials on cultures around the world. At Intercultural Press, materials are available for teachers who wish to enhance their understanding of cultural differences and explore strategies to use within the classroom.

Time, Continuity, and Change

Social studies programs should include experiences that provide for the study of the ways human beings view themselves in and over time.

Human beings seek to understand their historical roots and to locate themselves in time. Such understanding involves knowing what things were like in the past, how things have changed and developed, and how life might be different in the future. Knowing how to read and reconstruct the past encourages students to develop a historical perspective and determine how the world has changed and how it might change over time. The study of time, continuity, and change in respect to human culture includes the following:

- Perspectives from various aspects of history
- Historical knowledge of social issues
- The habits of mind that historians and scholars in the humanities and social sciences employ to study the past and its relationship to the present in the United States and other societies

Through this study of time, continuity, and change, students begin to recognize that individuals and cultures may hold different views regarding the past; therefore, they understand the relationships between human decisions and the resulting consequences. They also begin to understand and appreciate differences in historical perspectives, recognizing that interpretations are influenced by individual experiences, societal values, and cultural traditions.

As students learn these concepts of time, continuity, and change, they come to realize that culture is fluid and that history is affected by national interdependence, natural and manmade tragedies, and reconfigured boundaries. Merryfield (in press) suggests that one way to help students understand the issue of culture fluidity is by having them look at the experiences of people across three generations. Just as the culture of the United States has changed greatly from the early part of the twentieth century to the early part of the twenty-first, the culture of all other countries has changed as well. Unfortunately, students often have a view of other cultures as they were at a specific point in history.

For students to understand that places and people change over time, they should be given the opportunity to investigate how cities and other locations have evolved through the years. Several websites provide a glimpse of how cities looked hundreds of years ago, and they compare the streets and major areas with their modern counterparts. Sydney Streets provides a view of how the city of Sydney, Australia, has changed during the past two hundred years. Two trade books that show the evolution of cities and streets over time are *A City through Time* and *A Street through Time* by Steve Noon.

People, Places, and Environments

Social studies programs should include experiences that provide for the study of people, places, and environments.

Technological advances have begun to connect students to the world beyond their personal locations. The study of people, places, and human/environmental interactions assists students as they create their spatial views and geographic perspectives of the world. Geographic concepts are central to the comprehension of global connections for learners as they expand their knowledge of diverse cultures, both historical and contemporary. Core geographic themes are significant in reference to public policy and should be explored by students as they investigate issues of domestic and international importance.

As teachers prepare to teach in regard to people and places, Global Learning Online provides the following list of issues that should be considered:

- What are the goals and objectives for teaching about this place?
- What knowledge beyond the textbook is available regarding the economic situation, basic geography, religion, languages, and other issues related to this country?

- What resources are available to further the teacher's understanding of the country?
- What images and stereotypes do the students hold concerning this country? How can the curriculum be used to overcome these stereotypes?
- Do the materials available represent the views of the people who live in this country?
- What teaching strategies will enable the students to identify with the experiences of the citizens of this country?
- Does instruction focus on the people or the place?
- What personal experiences can the teacher use as a part of instruction?
- How comfortable would the teacher feel if a teacher from this country were a "fly on the wall" in the classroom?
- Are the materials presented primary sources, including works and images from those who make this place their home?
- Are ordinary life experiences and social issues presented about the people who live in this country, or is the focus only on the exotic?
- Are controversial issues included?

One strategy for teaching about a location is a cyber field trip. This can be done through a virtual field trip or through the Internet. There are many sites that feature these live, interactive expeditions around the world. These sites provide a comprehensive view that enhances students' understanding. Hundreds of virtual field trips can be found at TechTrekers and at Teachnology Virtual Field Trips.

Individual Development and Identity

Social studies programs should include experiences that provide for the study of individual development and identity.

Personal identity is shaped by one's culture, by outside groups, and by institutional influences. Given the nature of individual development and the impact of cultural norms, students need to be aware of the processes of learning, growth, and development that affect them on a personal level and understand that these factors also affect the development of students across the world. Students are encouraged to identify the variety of ways in which family, religion, gender, ethnicity, nationality, socioeconomic status, and other group and cultural influences contribute to the development of a sense of self.

Trade books are a valuable source for helping students understand their own development and the kinship they share with students around the world. This is especially true of multicultural trade books. Trade books provide links among cultures and offer an appropriate vehicle for engaging the sensibilities of students, meeting geographic goals, and aiding in the development of global awareness. Through trade books, students can develop social sensitivity to the needs of others and thereby realize that people have similarities as well as differences. They also can gain aesthetic appreciation of the artistic contributions of people from many cultural backgrounds.

The NCSS and the Children's Book Council have created annotated book lists for student use. Books selected for this bibliography are written primarily for children in grades K–8. The selection committee suggests that multicultural trade books should do the following:

- Emphasize human relations
- Represent a diversity of groups
- Be sensitive to a broad range of cultural experiences
- Present an original theme or a fresh slant on a traditional topic
- Be easily readable and of high literary quality
- Have a pleasing format and, when appropriate, illustrations that enrich the text
- Offer a factual, realistic, and balanced treatment of issues
- Focus on interactions among racial/minority groups and the dominant culture
- Avoid stereotypes
- Promote the value of diversity through illustrations, characterizations, and setting

Individuals, Groups, and Institutions

Social studies programs should include experiences that provide for the study of interactions among individuals, groups, and institutions.

It is important that students know how groups and institutions are formed, what controls and influences them, how they control and influence individuals and culture, and how they can be maintained or changed. Students should be assisted in recognizing the tensions that occur when the goals, values, and principles of two or more institutions or groups are in conflict. This understanding often comes through the interactions between individuals or groups of individuals from varied backgrounds.

Modern technology allows students to communicate directly with other people around the world. Geography, history, politics, and world culture become more relevant to students as they communicate directly with their counterparts in distant locations. Through Internet videoconferencing and e-mail exchanges, students can receive first-person accounts of how others live their lives.

Student e-mail is an important tool for teaching and learning, enabling students to exchange ideas and writings with partner schools in other countries. These e-mail connections by students are referred to by different names, such as key pals, e-pals, or Web pals. ePALS Classroom Exchange connects users from around the globe, providing the tools and meeting places to create a worldwide community of learners.

Kidlink is based on the idea that enabling students around the world to talk to each other will allow them a direct experience with students sharing the common experiences of childhood. Kidlink encourages students to consider differing opinions and to use these new ideas as a means to gain better insights into all views concerning a particular issue. Kidlink allows students to make friends, create social networks, and collaborate with peers around the world through e-mail, live chats, and discussion groups.

Although the idea of communication via e-mail or a live chat with students of the same age in other countries would seemingly lead to better cultural understanding, there are many potential problems. Before beginning an Internet project allowing direct communications between students, planning is critical. If classroom instruction and discussion regarding the other country has not occurred, trivial discussions that fail to lead to enhanced understanding may be generated. The questions or comments may appear rude or insulting and may actually reinforce stereotypes. The teacher should screen messages before they are sent. Adequate research and study regarding the country beforehand can eliminate most of these problems.

Power, Authority, and Governance

Social studies programs should include experiences that provide for the study of how people create and change structures of power, authority, and governance.

By examining structures of power, authority, and governance, students develop an understanding of how groups and nations attempt to resolve conflicts and establish order and security. Through studying the dynamic relationships among individual rights and responsibilities, the needs of social groups, and the concepts of a just society, learners become more effective problem solvers and decision makers when addressing the persistent issues and social problems encountered in public life.

These complex concepts can be taught at every grade level. Angel and Avery (1992) note that most elementary teachers are keenly aware that global issues are already a part of young students' daily experiences both inside and outside of school. The equitable distribution of limited resources, consumption, waste management, discrimination, and conflict are regular issues in the elementary classroom. Through instruction in social studies, students recognize that the problems they experience in and out of school are a reflection of the larger global problems of aggression, overpopulation, resource depletion, pollution, poverty, and human rights inequities. This recognition is the first step in dealing with problems that will become increasingly more complex as they mature.

As students progress to middle and high schools, the goals of social studies classes should be for students to accomplish the following:

- Understand that America has never existed in a vacuum and that events occurring within its borders affect other people
- Realize that the unanimity of decision making is rare
- Recognize that national interests color historical interpretations

Reaching these goals will strengthen the globalization, internationalization, and critical thinking aspects of social studies (Garil, 2000).

Production, Distribution, and Consumption

Social studies programs should include experiences that provide for the study of how people organize for the production, distribution, and consumption of goods and services.

People have wants that often exceed the limited resources available to them. As a result, the unequal distribution of resources necessitates systems of exchange. These systems of exchanges are becoming increasingly global in scope and require the systematic study of an interdependent world economy along with the role of technology in economic decision making. Understanding these systems of exchange begins with students looking at how they personally exchange goods and money.

Elementary students begin to understand the concepts of production, distribution, and consumption by learning to differentiate between wants and needs. This can begin by having students solve problems involving limited resources. As students work on these problems, Angel and Avery (1992) suggest that two considerations are necessary. First, issues should be presented as genuinely problematic. Materials designed for global education at the elementary level are often aimed at simply building awareness of international problems. Teachers should, however, engage secondary students in examining the related causes and consequences of those realities. Although young children cannot understand all the variables related to the politics concerning an issue, they can begin to recognize that conflicting opinions exist.

Second, students should be given opportunities for decision making and social action. As young people explore the ways in which global issues affect their lives, they need to feel that they can contribute to positive, meaningful change. Data generated, collected, and organized by the students is particularly meaningful in helping students understand the issues behind the distribution of the earth's resources. A meaningful activity is described in And My World, a curricular unit developed by the 4-H International Curriculum Committee. In this activity, students try to use only 1.5 gallons of water for one day (the amount used by the majority of the people in the world) and record how they use the allocated supply.

Science, Technology, and Society

Social studies programs should include experiences that provide for the study of relationships among science, technology, and society.

This standard is more interdisciplinary than the others, allowing students to see how social issues, science, government, and technology are interwoven. Although societal, scientific, and governmental issues have been studied in social studies classes for generations, the effect of technology on these issues is new to this generation of students. Today's technology forms the basis for some of society's most difficult choices. It will be up to this generation of students to determine how they can manage technology so that the greatest number of people benefit from it. It will also be up to them to determine how technology can make the world a technologically linked global village.

By exploring broad global issues and being involved in resolving global problems, students come to understand the complex issues that make up any global dispute. An effective strategy for developing a sense of the multidimensional nature of global issues is for students to track an issue as it emerges in the news and then to explore the issue from a variety of vantage points.

It is important that this tracking include the use of primary resources. The use of primary sources, such as newspapers and newsletters, as an investigative tool by students is a way to achieve an objective approach to a global perspective in the content areas. Such an investigation promotes higher-order thinking and communication skills. In using primary sources, students must decide if the source is truly valid and reliable, in what context of time and circumstances it was used, and what group or person created the document. The Library of Congress, along with other sources, is an excellent site for primary sources. Major newspapers across the world are available online with translations into English as well.

Another site of special interest for the latest global news is Global Express. The aim of Global Express is to enable students to gain a greater understanding of news stories from the developing world and the context in which they happen. This allows students to build links between their own life experiences and their understanding of global issues. This site provides classroom materials that help answer student questions and provoke discussion in the classroom. Its purpose is to increase student awareness of how media can influence their image of the developing world.

Global Connections

Social studies programs should include experiences that provide for the study of global connections and interdependence.

The focus of Standard Nine is on understanding global connections, but as shown throughout this chapter, it is virtually impossible to teach social studies without dealing with the global issues that affect students' lives. The realities of the twenty-first century require that students understand the increasingly important and diverse global connections among world societies. Therefore, teachers of social studies should provide developmentally appropriate experiences designed so that students can accomplish the following:

- Understand how language, art, music, belief systems, and other cultural elements impact global understanding
- Recognize conditions and motivations that contribute to conflict, co-operation, and interdependence among groups, societies, and nations
- Appreciate the effects of changing technologies on the global community
- Understand the causes, consequences, and possible solutions to persistent, contemporary, and emerging global issues, such as health care, security, resource allocation, economic development, and environmental quality
- Recognize the relationships and tensions between national sovereignty and global interests in such matters as territorial disputes, economic development, nuclear and other weapons deployment, use of natural resources, and human rights concerns
- Demonstrate an understanding of concerns, standards, issues, and conflicts related to universal human rights
- Appreciate how individual behaviors and decisions connect with global systems

These objectives can be met at every grade level. In the early grades, the students can come to understand that people across the world share a need for housing, family, friends, education, and religion. The focus is on commonalities, not differences. As students progress, they come to understand the problems that can arise when differing beliefs and values come into conflict. At the secondary level, students begin to understand the impact of personal, national, and global decisions and interactions.

Civic Ideals and Practices

Social studies programs should include experiences that provide for the study of the ideals, principles, and practices of citizenship in a democratic republic.

An understanding of civic ideals and practices of citizenship is critical to full participation in society and is a central purpose of social studies in the United States. This involves the explicit and continuing study of the basic concepts and values that underlie the democratic form of government. This also encompasses the understanding that citizens of the United States are also citizens of the world and that with this citizenship comes obligations both to the United States and to the planet at large.

This wider component of civic education requires that students acquire the knowledge and skills to participate more effectively in local, state, national, and international affairs. This development necessitates civic attention on a transnational and transcultural scale. It goes beyond students simply knowing that they are citizens of the world, extending to an acknowledgment of their responsibilities both to each other and to the earth itself. Global citizenship requires the desire and ability to tackle injustice and inequality on every level. Civic responsibility at the local and global levels can begin in the early grades with participation in community service and service projects, which can lead to a belief that students can make a difference.

During the presidential elections of 2004, educators were able to teach students about the concepts of citizenship, civic responsibility, democracy, and the importance of political participation through a project called Kids Voting USA. This program allowed students to participate in an authentic voting experience as children across the United States cast a ballot on election day, voting on the same candidates and issues as adults.

CONCLUSION

The NCSS provides an opportunity for students to see beyond their local community to the outside world. Merryfield (in press) has identified the following eleven research-based strategies that should be considered as teachers provide a globally oriented social studies curriculum:

1. Teachers must help students develop a local/global connection. Students must come to see themselves as part of a larger world. Their communities are influenced by the actions and beliefs of people around the world.
2. Teachers must help students develop perspective consciousness and the ability to have multiple perspectives. Students must learn that people differ in how they see and value events and issues. Students must come to understand that there are often many sides to an issue and that no one answer might be the correct one.
3. Teachers must present the world as a system. Students need to see their lives and community as part of a larger political, economic, and environmental system.
4. Teachers must teach about global issues. Therefore, students come to understand that issues that impact another part of the world are their problems as well.
5. Teachers must help students recognize power in a global context. They come to understand that major decision makers may not be local or national governments but multinational corporations or nongovernmental organizations that have control over political decisions.
6. Teachers must help students recognize nonstate actors, such as individuals, corporations, multinational organizations, and nongovernmental organizations. These groups often affect local, national, and global events and issues.
7. Teachers must help students develop tolerance for those different than they. Students need to recognize their personal prejudices and stereotypes. They must come to understand how these prejudices and stereotypes can lead to injustices and inequalities.
8. Teachers must help students develop the ability to communicate and interact with individuals from cultures different from their own.

9. Teachers must provide opportunities for students to develop and use research and thinking skills. Students must learn to seek information from a variety of sources and to evaluate the merit and worth of these sources.
10. Teachers must encourage students to participate in local and global service projects.
11. Teachers must provide opportunities for student to use electronic technologies.

Perhaps the greatest lesson learned while studying from a global perspective is that the answers to most of life's most perplexing problems are not found in textbooks. Unlike social studies topics of the past for which the answers were typically found somewhere in the textbook, global issues represent unanswered questions. Looking beyond local concerns, personal prejudices, and stereotypes and viewing oneself as a citizen of the world is the only way that students will find the solutions to these global problems and issues. This, surely, is the most important lesson we can share with our students.

INSTRUCTIONAL IDEAS

Integrating Social Studies and Web-Based Lessons

Featured on CNN, The Geography Olympics website consists of two parts: activities dealing with Geography Facts and the Geography Olympics. The Geography Facts area contains information pertinent to over twenty-five commonly asked world geography questions, including How old is the earth? How many countries are there in the world? and What are the deepest parts of the ocean? Information from this area of the site is quite useful for helping students grasp the big picture of the world in which they live.

The Geography Olympics area contains an interactive geography challenge. Students may join the challenge in support of their country by selecting which country they will be representing and taking the quiz. The quiz consists of trying to locate ten randomly selected countries on a map of the world. The quiz is different every time it is played, and students may take it up to three times per day. The main Web page contains a leaderboard that reports the countries that are in first, second, and third place as well as a link to the full leaderboard with the ranking of each of the almost 200 participating countries.

The page also links to a U.S. leaderboard that indicates the rank of each individual state. Students may take the quiz as many times as they wish to try to improve their state and/or country ranking, and all the while they are learning and practicing world geography!

Integrating Social Studies and Multimedia Presentations

The Lonely Planet is an organization that defines itself as "passionate about bringing people together, about understanding our world, and about people sharing experiences that enrich everyone's lives." It provides in-depth information about every corner of the world and accepts no endorsements, advertising, or payment for its information or its reviews.

By clicking on the Worldguide link at this site, students encounter a colorful, interactive map of the world. They can select a region and then a specific country within that region, or they can choose to go directly to a country's site. Once a country has been selected, a detailed map appears that includes cities, geographic areas, attractions, and other places of interest. Each place on the map is fully interactive and takes the students to another page containing detailed information about the spot. In addition to general information about the area, the site also includes a slide show of pictures from the area.

Students researching different areas of the world will find all the information they need at this site. The maps, images, and detailed descriptions provide students with plenty of resources for creating a variety of multimedia presentations.

Integrating Social Studies and Telecomputing Projects

Postcard Geography is a simple, annual, worldwide telecomputing project that is open to classes with students of all age levels. On registration, classes commit to exchanging postcards with all other registered participants. Students create or select a class postcard that depicts their locale, provide information about their class and their culture, and prepare to mail them to all other classes on their list. The project becomes exciting and rewarding for students as they begin to receive postcards in the mail from the other participating classes.

This activity provides students of all ages with experiences using maps and globes, determining the distance cards have traveled, or implementing guessing contests for longest distance traveled, card received from the community closest to theirs, and so on. Students can also create a database of participants in their category. The cultural exchange can be extended by selecting classrooms for additional e-mail or ongoing curricular collaboration. This project can be a wonderful introduction to students from all over the world!

Integrating Social Studies and Online Discussions

The Global Nomads Group (GNG) is a an organization that fosters dialogue and understanding among the world's youth. Founded in 1998, GNG uses interactive technologies such as videoconferencing to "bring young people together face-to-face to meet across cultural and national boundaries to discuss their differences and similarities, and the world issues that affect them." By participating in these activities, students improve their communication skills, geography skills, and critical thinking skills and develop a deeper level of cultural understanding.

Registered classes receive information about various GNG programs through an e-mail newsletter. The programs change periodically to address current events in the world. An example is Project Voice, an activity that took place on March 3, 2003, just days before the U.S.-led invasion of Iraq. The participants, a small group of Iraqi high school students from Baghdad College and American students from the Metropolitan Learning Center in Connecticut, met through videoconference to discuss their daily lives, their respective cultures, their hopes and dreams for the future, and their views on the approaching war. Examples of other GNG projects include an ongoing activity dealing with the Israeli–Palestinian conflict and the crisis in Sudan, the latter including a firsthand account of the Breijing Refugee Camp.

INTERNET RESOURCES

And My World: http://www.oznet.ksu.edu/library/4h_y2/samplers/4H635.asp
ePALS Classroom Exchange: http://www.epals.com/
Exworthy Educational Resources: http://members.tripod.com/exworthy/cult.htm
The Geography Olympics: http://www.geographyolympics.com/challenge.php

Global Express: http://atschool.eduweb.co.uk/rmext05/glo/aims.html
Global Learning Online: http://atschool.eduweb.co.uk/rmext05/glo/index.html
Global Nomads Group: http://www.gng.org/home.html
Intercultural Press: http://www.interculturalpress.com/shop/home.html
Kidlink: http://www.kidlink.org/english/general/index.html
Kids Voting USA: http://www.kidsvotingusa.org/default.asp
Library of Congress: http://lcweb.loc.gov
The Lonely Planet: http://www.lonelyplanet.com/
National Council for the Social Studies and the Children's Book Council
    http://www.socialstudies.org/resources/notable/
Postcard Geography: http://pcg.cyberbee.com/index.html
Sydney Streets: http://www.cityofsydney.nsw.gov.au/history/sydneystreets/
    Then_&_Now/default.html
Teachnology Virtual Field Trips: http://www.teach-nology.com/teachers/
    field_trips/virtual/
TechTrekers: http://www.techtrekers.com/virtualft.htm

REFERENCES

Angel, A. V., & Avery, P. G. (1992). Examining global issues in the elementary classroom. *The Social Studies*, *83*, 113–117.

Garil, B. A. (2000). U.S. social studies in the 21st century: Internationalizing the curriculum for global citizens. *The Social Studies*, *91*, 257–273.

Gilliom, M. E. (1981). Global education and the social studies. *Theory into Practice*, *20*, 169–173.

Merryfield, M. M. (in press). The many dimensions of global education. In M. M. Merryfield and A. Wilson (Eds.), *Global perspectives in the social studies*. Silver Spring, MD: National Council for the Social Studies.

National Council for the Social Studies. (1982). Position statement on global education. *Social Education*, *46*, 36–38.

National Council for the Social Studies. (1994). *Expectations of excellence: Curriculum standards for social studies*. Silver Spring, MD: NCSS. http://www.socialstudies.org/standards/

National Council for the Social Studies. (2001). *Preparing citizens for a global community—A position statement of National Council for the Social Studies*. Retrieved from http://www.socialstudies.org/positions/global/

CHAPTER 7

Global Education and Science

The earth will continue to regenerate its life sources only as long
as we and all the peoples of the world do our part to conserve its
natural resources. It is a responsibility which every human being
shares. Through voluntary action, each of us can join in building a
productive land in harmony with nature.

—Gerald Ford, former president of the United States,
discussing Earth Day, 1975

The interdependent relationship between science, the earth, and its inhabitants suggests a natural connection in a global curriculum. This
blending of scientific, global, and cultural studies seems logical since
much of what is known regarding ancient cultures and the history of the
earth comes from scientific evidence. Scientific research and technological advances support scientists in their pursuit of information dealing
with the history of our planet and enable them to make discoveries that
can affect the future of humanity as a whole. The future of the world depends to a large degree on scientific knowledge and the extent of its use.

When science is envisioned as a thread that is woven throughout the
global curriculum, today's students will better understand how to make
wise use of scientific knowledge as they make decisions that have a
global impact. When educators consider that the ideal global curriculum
is one integrated with science, learning becomes centered on and easily
transferable to real-life situations. This approach is one that provides students with the experiences and instruction necessary for developing a
view of themselves as world citizens—that their actions as individuals or
members of a group affect the world environment as a whole.

Within the science curriculum, Pike and Selby (1999) suggest the environment be considered as four interconnected areas, each with a different focus:

1. The natural environment of plants, animals, earth, air, and water
2. The man-made environment of artifacts humans build—tools, engines, machines, and structures
3. The group environment of cultures and other social units as well as the interdependent grouping of humans, plants, and animals
4. The inner environment of self-awareness within these surroundings

Effective environmental study can be discovered when viewing these four different environments from personal, local, national, and global perspectives.

FOUR AREAS OF ENVIRONMENTAL STUDY

An example of a learning activity that can be integrated across the four distinct areas of environmental study is Creating Continents, Climates, and Cultures. This teacher-created unit was designed to help students make cognitive connections between physical land formations, climate patterns, and the development of cultures that result from the interaction among these different features. Students use the Internet to compile information that will enable them to do the following:

- Explain relationships between physical land formations, climate patterns, and cultures
- Analyze the organization of people, places, and environments on the earth's surface
- Increase knowledge and understanding of the characteristics, distribution, and details of earth's cultural diversity

While this activity broadly connects the areas of science education in a global curriculum, other curricular activities address each of the four areas of environmental study identified by Pike and Selby (1999) more specifically.

Natural Environment

A study of the natural environment helps students realize that people everywhere have the same basic needs for sun, water, food, and air. The website of the Missouri Botanical Garden offers in-depth information regarding the world's ecosystems. Links from the home page take users to sites regarding the biomes of the rain forest, the tundra, the taiga, the desert, the temperate deciduous forest, and the grasslands. Additional links access information regarding the freshwater ecosystems of wetlands, rivers and streams, and ponds and lakes as well as the marine ecosystems of shorelines, temperate oceans, and tropical oceans.

Each of the site's sections is laid out in a similar fashion, enabling students to easily compare and contrast important aspects of these natural environments, including plant and animal life, climate, and terrain. Additional information allows students to discover threats to the ecosystems and strategies currently being implemented to protect them. All the areas provide beautiful photographs, and some even offer virtual field trips. A website such as this helps upper elementary and middle school students comprehend the interdependent relationships of the living and nonliving components of the natural environment and why the protection of all environments is critical to a healthy world.

Another website that provides detailed information regarding ecosystems is the PBS site based on the program Earth on the Edge. This site provides information appropriate for middle and high school students and includes the basic ecosystems described previously as well as a link to the urban ecosystem. Although not considered a natural environment, the urban ecosystem faces threats similar to those faced by the forests, grasslands, farms, rivers, and reefs. Also included at this site is an interactive quiz for students to test their knowledge regarding the earth's ecosystems.

Man-Made Environment

Studies of the human influence on the environment draw attention to the rapid advancements in science, technology, communication, and transportation that in turn have prompted a movement focused on the relationships between science, technology, and society. The basic premise of this movement is the exploration of the many ways science and technology affect culture and how modern cultures affect the way we study science and technology. Merryfield (1991) identified seven global issues, illustrated in Table 7.1, that combine the elements of science, technology, and society with topics in science education.

All seven of Merryfield's (1991) global issues are easily integrated into the science curriculum. One organization, the Population Reference Bureau (PRB), offers detailed information, lesson plans, and activities dealing with these issues. The PRB website provides timely and objective information on U.S. and international population trends and their worldwide implications. The following ideas for integrating the seven global issues into the science curriculum are based on information from this site, which contains data that are easy to understand and useful for upper elementary through high school students:

Environmental: US in the World is a project designed to help Americans explore how a shared concern for the environment connects peo-

Table 7.1   Seven Elements of Science Education Involved with Global Issues. Source: Merryfield (1991).

Environmental This element addresses environmental issues caused by population growth and technologies.
Health and Population This element addresses the health care problems created by exploding populations.
Economic This element addresses standards of living that provide basic human needs of food, clothing, shelter, health care, education, security, and leisure.
Transportation and Communication This element addresses problems of unequal access to technology and swift means of transportation.
Food and Hunger This element addresses the unequal distribution and location of food sources.
Energy This element involves the search for sources of energy that do not harm the environment.
Military Issues This element addresses fear and the consequences of the global trade of weapons of mass destruction.

ple in the United States to people in other parts of the world. The project includes a series of fact sheets that compare trends in the United States with those in developing countries and demonstrates how population structure, growth, and dynamics can lead to environmental devastation and threaten human well-being in both locations.

Health and population: Food for Thought is a spatial graphing activity that uses the participants as part of the graph. The activity helps students develop a sense of the similarities and differences between populations. Many measures are used for comparison, including population, population density, population growth rates, life expectancy, and energy consumption. A detailed lesson plan is followed with extension activities and ideas for modifying the activity for lower grades.

Economic: The website Human Population: Fundamentals of Growth Environmental Relationships describes how people's lifestyles, consumption patterns, and the regions they inhabit and use directly affect the environment. This Web page deals with issues concerning food insecurity, inadequate sanitation, water supplies, and housing and an inability to meet the basic needs of the current population. Also included are a teacher's guide and related Internet links.

Transportation and communication: Often students do not realize how dependent our society has become on transportation and communication. They also are not aware of the hardships faced by people without access to these conveniences. Many people in the United States and worldwide do not have any means of transportation, so that getting to work, running errands, and picking up children from day care can be a daily struggle. The PRB article "The Toll on Rural Commuters" can be used as a discussion starter for middle and high school students regarding unequal access to transportation, communication, and technology.

Food and hunger: The population of the world reached 6 billion in 1999. Although no one knows exactly where or when that 6 billionth child was born, The World of the Child 6 Billion project looks at the concerns that children of this generation will face. The discussion guide highlights the basic needs of people worldwide and gives examples of projects that are helping to meet these needs in Burkina Faso, Indonesia, the Dominican Republic, Botswana, Bolivia, and Laos.

Energy: The brochure Critical Links: Population, Health, and the Environment, published by the PRB, takes an in-depth look at the world production of fossil fuel and the energy usage per capita in different world regions. The environmental energy requirements of the world's 6.3 billion people are unprecedented. The fundamental relationships are easy for students to comprehend: earth provides energy and raw materials for human activities, and those activities generate pollution and damage to environmental resources, in the process harming human health and well-being. Students and teachers can use this brochure to study the environmental effects of different forms of energy and to research new, less harmful forms of energy.

Military issues: "Conflict Chips Away at Living Conditions in the Sudan" is an article published on the PRB website that deals with the costs of war on the native Sudanese people. Hopes for peace have stalled in this country, in which war has displaced whole communities and destroyed basic services. Although some students recognize human causalities as a by-product of war, many do not realize the economic, environmental, and medical strains that are placed on the citizens of countries at war. This article can be used as a discussion starter for middle and high school students and can be integrated into the social studies curriculum as well.

Group Environment

Classroom teachers might begin their instruction with a study of how the environment of specific groups is affected by the daily activities of people around the planet. The World Wildlife Fund is a worldwide conservation organization whose website offers teachers and students facts and activities that enable them to find information regarding conservation and its role in their lives, to research endangered species, to tackle environmental issues, and to recognize the principles of evolution. This comprehensive website offers extensive information regarding the habitats and species of the world as well as interactive games and activities for students in intermediate through high school grades.

Another excellent resource for researching environmental topics regarding specific cultures or groups is the World Resources Institute, an independent nonprofit organization with a staff of scientists, economists, policy experts, business analysts, statistical analysts, mapmakers, and communicators who work to protect the earth and improve people's lives. The World Resources Institute website provides information regarding the many ways the organization is making a difference in the global environment.

Earthtrends is the online database of the World Resources Institute that focuses on the environmental, social, and economic trends that shape the world and that provides information from a wide variety of global data sources. The data at Earthtrends are divided into the following ten categories:

1. Coastal and marine ecosystems
2. Water resources and freshwater ecosystems
3. Climate and atmosphere
4. Population, health, and human well-being
5. Economics, business, and the environment
6. Energy and resources
7. Biodiversity and protected areas
8. Agriculture and food
9. Forests, grasslands, and drylands
10. Environmental governance and institutions

The collected information for each of these topics can be accessed through a searchable database, data tables, country profiles, maps, and features. Previously, much of this information was inaccessible or difficult to locate, but this site provides free and easy access for students researching the interaction between humans and the different categories of the global environment. For example, a student researching the consumption of paper products in different parts of the world can access the Earthtrends database, select the energy and resources link, select the link for resource consumption of paper, and select the countries or regions to compare, at which point the database will generate a list of the requested information. Middle and high school students can effectively use this information to determine relationships between the four interconnected areas of the environment.

Inner Environment

An important aspect of global awareness is students' realization of their own responsibilities for improving and protecting the quality of the earth's natural resources. A nonprofit organization dedicated to researching and protecting the environment is the Union of Concerned Scientists (UCS). Faculty members and students at the Massachusetts Institute of Technology who were concerned about the misuse of science and technology in society founded this organization in 1969. The goal of the UCS is to ensure that all people have clean air, energy, and transportation as well as food that is produced in a safe and sustainable manner. The UCS strives to ensure that our planet supports a rich diversity of life and seeks to improve humanity's stewardship of the earth.

A section of the UCS website is Greentips, an online source for putting environmental ideas into action. Recent articles include topics such as what to do with old electronics, risk-free pest control, and ideas for cleaner and greener home improvement. Students of all ages can research the Greentips articles to discover ways to improve the environment by making changes in their own lives.

Also located at the UCS site is the interactive Great Green Web Game. Appropriate for students of all grade levels, this game tests their knowledge of how consumer choices affect the environment. Students travel around a traditional-looking online game board as they answer questions and "shop green." As they play, the Envirometer gauges the cumulative impact of their choices. The center point on the Envirometer game board represents the impact of an average American household on the environment, and at the end of the game students can compare this average to their own impact on air quality, water quality, natural habitats, and the sustainability of the climate.

MULTIDISCIPLINARY ACTIVITIES

Science resources related to global education can be integrated into other areas of the curriculum as well, and one area that particularly lends itself to integration across the disciplines is the study and celebration of Earth Day. Earth Day is a worldwide effort begun in 1970 that focuses on global issues regarding the environment, its resources, and related problems. Over the years, Earth Day has evolved into a global endeavor to focus attention on earth's environmental problems within schools and communities throughout the world. The Earth Day curriculum website contains links to many activities and lessons useful for teaching math, language arts, social studies, and fine arts with an environmental focus, including the following:

Cleaning Up for Earth Day: A math activity where students collect garbage and then graph the results.

What Can I Do?: An Earth Day story followed by comprehension questions.

Rainforest Poetry: Lesson plans for students to develop different forms of poetry that reflect their knowledge of rainforest issues.

There's an Owl in the Shower: Students gather facts on old-growth forests and the logging industry from reading *There's an Owl in the Shower*, gather facts about the spotted owl in the Pacific Northwest, and write a persuasive essay, taking one side of the issue.

Save Trees by Making Your Own Recycled Paper: Students learn the importance of recycling and how to make recycled paper.

The Earth Day Network is a chief organization influencing environmental awareness around the world. Through the Earth Day Network, individuals and groups connect, interact, and impact their communities, creating positive change in local, national, and global policies. The Earth Day Network's international network reaches more than 12,000 organizations in 174 countries, and through the U.S. program, more than 3,000 groups and 100,000 educators coordinate community development and environmental protection activities throughout the year. Earth Day is celebrated on April 22 of each year by more than half a billion people of all backgrounds, faiths, and nationalities. The Earth Day Network provides a wide variety of lessons for students in kindergarten through high school. Examples of online lesson plans for celebrating Earth Day and teaching sustainability include the following:

Food and You: Designed to incorporate environmental education into general math and science classes for elementary school classes (kindergarten to fifth grade), this lesson encourages students to think about where their food comes from, the food production process, and the by-products associated with their favorite foods.

The Trash We Pass: Middle school students (fourth to seventh grade) in social studies, math, and science classes analyze garbage and recycling options.

Have and Have-Not: Middle school students (seventh to ninth grade) in social studies, geography, math, and economics classes gain a perspective on different consumption habits in developing and developed countries and the effect that mass consumption has on the ecological footprint of a country and of an individual.

Sustainable Dining: Lower high school students (seventh to tenth grade) in economics, home economics, and general education classes learn about sustainably produced groceries as a valuable and environmentally friendly option for grocery shopping.

Renewable Energy: High school history, science, and math students analyze the use of energy in their everyday lives and consider the advantages and disadvantages of environmentally friendly renewable energy sources.

Another resource for multidisciplinary activities is *Green Teacher*, a magazine that can be used by educators to enhance environmental and global education across the curriculum at all grade levels. Archived articles from the magazine are available at the website with instructional ideas for Earth Day and the rest of the year. The articles also include ideas for rethinking education with regard to environmental and global problems; reports of what successful teachers, parents, and other youth educators are doing; cross-curricular activities for various grade levels; and evaluations of new books, kits, games, and other resources.

A source for ideas for multidisciplinary activities and lessons with trade books is the Education World website. An article at the website includes reviews of five picture books that examine the relationship between humans and nature from a global perspective and can be used across the reading and science curriculums:

- *One Less Fish* by Kim Michelle Toft and Allan Sheather describes the impact of humans on the world's coral reefs.
- *Jaguar* by Helen Cowcher is the story of a hunter who discovers the tracks of a jaguar but after stalking his prey realizes that the land belongs to the jaguar as much as to him.
- *A Closer Look at the Rainforest* by Selina Wood describes the threats and potential of the rainforest and includes tips for readers who want to help ensure the rainforest's survival.

- *Our Wet World* by Sneed B. Collard III and James M. Needham examines the wide variety of water ecosystems that are home to many species.
- *Common Ground: The Water, Earth, and Air We Share* by Molly Bang details what might happen to the earth if environmental abuse continues.

GLOBALIZING THE SCIENCE CURRICULUM IN K–12 CLASSROOMS

When is the appropriate entry point for students to study earth sustainability and the world's environmental problems? Although some teachers believe that secondary school courses are the appropriate place, emphasizing issues and problems arising from humans' exploitation of the natural environment and the expansion of the man-made environment, others believe that the correct question is not "when" but rather "how" a globalized curriculum is integrated into the classroom. The proper issue of readiness should deal with how the content principles, relationships, and global processes should be studied first from a broader, general context and then move to specifics, investigating concentrated, singular issues in depth.

The Elementary School Science Position Statement of the National Science Teachers Association (2004) stated that science instruction for elementary students should emphasize the following:

- Inquiry-based, hands-on activities
- Content presented in broad themes
- Mathematics and science integrated in the instruction as well as other disciplines
- A variety of instructional modes, allowing for different learning styles
- Group interaction
- Activities that integrate global issues and concerns

Taking these recommendations into consideration, science instruction can begin with a broad view of learning regarding the environment in the study of how earth systems change. Such lessons would enable students to recognize the power and potential of science in shaping our earth.

Those educators who believe that the emphasis on global science education should begin in secondary grades present a reasonable argument regarding student interest at those grade levels. Many middle and high school students have a keen interest in natural or man-made disasters, such as earthquakes, tornadoes, hurricanes, epidemics, and nuclear accidents. Students' interests regarding these phenomena at their ages could lead to more in-depth study, with special emphasis on the global implications of these disasters. These interests will be especially heightened if the students had been introduced to global science issues at the elementary level.

The National Science Teachers Association's position statement Learning Conditions for High School Science (2004) stated that continuing science instruction for high school students should maintain the recommendations for elementary students. Additionally, high school students should have the following:

- The required space and equipment for a laboratory-oriented approach to science
- A safe place to work and learn that is related to the laboratory use
- Appropriate and adequate resources of supplies and equipment, including audiovisual, to support student learning

Secondary students studying science cannot simply memorize concepts; they must construct their own understandings. Typically, students do not learn everything regarding advanced science concepts all at one time; rather, they learn in a spiraling manner, learning a skeletal basis of the concept first and progressively building on that knowledge until there is a deeper and richer understanding. Teaching and learning science occur most effectively when students study a topic from every vantage point. This educational philosophy allows the students to investigate, report, and write creatively, all of which are activities that help students construct that deeper and richer understanding.

CONCLUSION

Educators can employ many instructional strategies to provide students with the information they need to comprehend science from a global perspective. Technology and, more specifically, the Internet enable teachers of all grade levels to successfully integrate such lessons into the curriculum and allow students to discover solutions to scientific problems through real-world problem solving. The projects and activities available on the Internet provide educators with an abundance of global science resources, ideas for hands-on learning activities, and projects for developing higher-level thinking skills.

INSTRUCTIONAL IDEAS

Integrating Science and Online Discussions

Although the term "global warming" is frequently used, many students do not fully comprehend the meaning of the term. Two websites available from the Environmental Protection Agency (EPA) provide information and activities suitable for students of all ages. The Global Warming Kids' Site offers students kid-friendly definitions of global warming, climate, weather, and the greenhouse effect. The site also includes information describing how the things people do in their daily lives send greenhouse gases into the air and what can be done to improve the earth's climate. The Environmental Kids' Club has interactive games and activities dealing with air, water, garbage and recycling, plants and animals, and caring for the environment.

While this site is appropriate for younger students, the EPA site is filled with helpful information for older students. Students of all ages can select the Ask EPA link to read through previously asked questions or to ask questions of their own. Experts at the EPA will answer students question either through personal e-mail or by posting the answers on the Frequently Asked Questions page.

Integrating Science and Multimedia Presentations

While American students often take good health for granted, young people in other parts of the world are not fortunate to have access to good health care. Access Excellence, through the National Health Museum, created a series of interactive problem-solving activities called Mystery Spots. Each of the activities describes a scenario that deals with the spread of a potentially dangerous disease somewhere in the world. The students, acting as detectives, must solve the mystery to stop the spread of the disease. The gamelike appeal of these activities does not mask the critical nature of the topic or the importance of good health care on a global level.

As a follow-up activity, students could research a disease that is having a global impact and create a mystery game using a format similar to the Mystery Spots. Students could create the games as Web pages and share them with others via the Internet.

Integrating Science and Web-Based Lessons

The World Wildlife Fund game Poacher Peril is a downloadable activity that puts players in the position of endangered animals and challenges them to try to outwit a deadly poacher. This interactive board game begins as up to four players try to stay a step ahead of the poachers. A roll of the dice determines players' and poachers' moves around the board, and players must answer questions regarding various rare animals as they play the game.

Students may choose to play the game as elephants, tigers, rhinos, or snow leopards. The questions asked and the information given throughout the game is based on information dealing with the selected animal, why it is being poached, and what is being done by the World Wildlife Fund and other organizations to protect the animal.

Players whose animals make it to the end of the game board (the nature preserve) are winners. The game is available in PC and Mac formats and is appropriate for students in the middle grades and high school.

Integrating Science and Telecomputing Projects

Among the many educational activities available at the Earth Day Network is the Ecological Footprint Quiz. Students answer fifteen easy questions based on four categories: food, goods and services, shelter, and mobility. They can then compare their Ecological Footprints to what other people use and to what is available on this planet. The results of this quiz estimate how much productive land and water you need to support what you use and what you discard.

As a telecomputing project, students can take the quiz individually and combine their scores for a class Ecological Footprint. Class scores can be shared and compared with the scores of other classes both in the United States and globally, and students can use the information available at the Earth Day Network website to determine how they might be able to reduce their Ecological Footprint scores. The main quiz is appropriate for middle through high school students, and Billy Bigfoot is a version of the quiz for younger students.

INTERNET RESOURCES

Billy Bigfoot: http://www.kidsfootprint.org/

Conflict Chips Away at Living Conditions in the Sudan by Yvette Collymore: http://www.prb.org/Template.cfm?Section=PRB&template=/ContentMan agement/ContentDisplay.cfm&ContentID=10630

Creating Continents, Climates, and Cultures: http://www.teachnetlab.org/ santab/mikeorton/Homepage.html/

Critical Links: Population, Health, and the Environment: http://www.prb.org/ Template.cfm?Section=PRB&template=/ContentManagement/Content Display.cfm&ContentID=9847

Earth Day: http://www.state.sd.us/deca/DDN4Learning/ThemeUnits/Earth-Day/index.htm

Earth Day Network: http://www.earthday.net/

Earth on the Edge: http://www.pbs.org/earthonedge/index.html

Earthtrends: http://earthtrends.wri.org/

Education World: http://www.educationworld.com/a_books/books042.shtml

Environmental Protection Agency: http://www.epa.gov/

Food for Thought: http://www.prb.org/Template.cfm?Section=LessonPlans &template=/ContentManagement/ContentDisplay.cfm&ContentID=5000

Great Green Web Game: http://www.ucsusa.org/game/game.html

Green Teacher: http://www.greenteacher.com/

Greentips: http://www.ucsusa.org

Missouri Botanical Garden: http://mbgnet.mobot.org/

Mystery Spots: http://www.accessexcellence.org/AE/mspot/

Poacher Peril: http://www.wwf.org.uk/poacherperil/

Population Reference Bureau: http://www.prb.org/

The Toll on Rural Commuters by Lori Nitschke: http://www.prb.org/ Template.cfm?Section=PRB&template=/ContentManagement/Content Display.cfm&ContentID=10204

Union of Concerned Scientists: http://www.ucsusa.org/

US in the World: http://www.prb.org/Content/NavigationMenu/PRB/Educators/ US_in_the_World/US_in_the_World.htm

The World of the Child 6 Billion: http://www.prb.org/Content/NavigationMenu/ PRB/Educators/Child_6_Billion/The_World_of_Child_6_Billion.htm

World Resources Institute: http://www.wri.org/

World Wildlife Fund: http://www.panda.org/

REFERENCES

Merryfield, M. M. (1991). Science-technology-society and global perspectives. *Theory into Practice, 30,* 288–293.

National Science Teachers Association. (2004). Elementary school position statement. Retrieved October 21, 2004, from http://www.nsta.org/ positionstatement&psid=8.

National Science Teachers Association. (2004). Position statement of learning conditions for high school science. Retrieved October 21, 2004, from http://www.ntsa.org/positionstatement&pside=38.

Pike, G., & Selby, D. (1999). *In the global classroom, book 1.* Toronto: Pippin Publishing.

CHAPTER 8

Global Education and Mathematics

If you are not part of the solution, you are part of the problem.

—Eldridge Cleaver, speech in San Francisco, 1968

When considering approaches for adding global perspectives to the curriculum, little attention is given to the subject area of mathematics. Perhaps this is because mathematics is considered a universal language that does not exist relative to national loyalties or personal beliefs. Mathematical truth is thought to transcend culture, and this perception of mathematics has led educators to feel it is unnecessary to add cultural or global perspectives to the mathematics curriculum.

After all, mathematics is the only language shared by all human beings regardless of their culture, religion, or gender. Mathematicians from widely varying cultural backgrounds have little difficulty communicating their mathematical results. The principles of mathematics hold true regardless of where they are taught. Determining the cost of products involves the same mathematical process regardless of whether the total is expressed in dollars, rubles, or pounds. Although it is true that pure mathematical processes are universal because they deal with nothing but numbers, cultural influences impact students' problem-solving skills when they are working with real-world mathematical problems.

Because of the view that the use of numbers and their related con cepts don't possess any global differences, mathematics is considered *acultural*, a discipline without cultural significance. However, no classroom or subject matter can be truly acultural.

As long as humans from varied backgrounds develop mathematical concepts, teach mathematics to the next generation of citizens, and learn mathematics so that they can function in a global society, mathematics cannot be viewed as acultural.

When mathematics is taught from an acultural perspective, students fail to learn how mathematics has evolved and who has contributed to this evolution. Students are taught that there is only one right way to construct the solving of a problem. They are required to assimilate procedures by rote without any personal or individual conceptualizing. All problems are the same regardless of a student's culture or country of origin. When viewed as acultural, mathematics is seen as a neutral subject area in which a student's background, culture, language, and heritage are detached from the curriculum.

This view obviously raises concerns for educators who value providing a global perspective to the teaching of mathematics. The National Council of Teachers of Mathematics (2000) expressed its position as to the place mathematics serves in today's world and the need that it be viewed as culturally influenced in the following statement:

> Mathematics is one of the greatest cultural and intellectual achievements of humankind, and citizens should develop an appreciation and understanding of this great achievement, including its aesthetic and even recreational aspects. (p. 4)

ETHNOMATHEMATICS

Ubiratan D'Ambrosio, a Brazilian mathematician, was the first to use the term *ethnomathematics*. D'Ambrosio (2001) describes ethnomathematics as the study of mathematics that takes into consideration the culture in which mathematics arises. The term *ethnomathematics* is used to express the relationship between culture and mathematics.

Ethnomathematics is a relatively recent field of studying mathematical representations from different cultural perspectives. Ethnomathematics expresses the relationship among mathematics, culture, education, and politics. The Greek term *ethnos* refers broadly to a person's nation of origin. In English, it has come to more specifically mean all the components that make up a culture: the traditions, language, food and dress, family life, values, beliefs, and physical characteristics. When placed together, *ethno* and *mathematics* are then a much broader consideration of the term *mathematics*, as ethnomathematics considers the varying ways this content area is used around the world (D'Ambrosio, 2001). The ethnomathematical perspective studies the number system and symbols of different ethnic groups and the representational systems of different aspect of their cultures.

The development of ethnomathematics has challenged the traditional concept of Euro-centered monorepresentational systems of mathematics and has been widely criticized. There are those who view ethnomathematics as an effort to be politically correct, and some have suggested that the approach "dumbs down" the math curriculum and gives teachers an excuse to avoid teaching math principles by encouraging students to talk about culture instead. When the *Chronicle of Higher Education* (2000) asked educators, "Is ethnomathematics a good thing? Will it attract more minority students to math? Does it pose risks to students' understanding of math?" the responses were heated and divided along two very distinct philosophical lines. Table 8.1 provides a review of the two views considering ethnomathematics.

Table 8.1   Philosophical Debate over Ethnomathematics. Source: *Chronicle of Higher Education*, October 6, 2000.

Arguments against Ethnomathematics	Arguments for Ethnomathematics
The beauty of mathematics is its purity; it is not tied to culture.	Anything that makes students "like" math is valuable.
Accuracy is sacrificed for political correctness.	It shows students that math is not separate from reality.
Ethnomathematics is the history of mathematics, not mathematics.	Ethnomathematics validates different ways of knowing.
There is no evidence that ethnomathematics increases math skills.	It encourages more black and Hispanic students to study and to do well in mathematics.
It does nothing to improving the student's grasp of the fundamental concepts; it is a distraction.	It allows and validates other ways of knowing.
Discipline and hard work are more important than ethnomathematics.	

UNIVERSAL MATH SKILLS

The application of math skills is similar in every culture (Mathematics Makes a World of Difference in Our Lives!, 2001). People everywhere use mathematics to solve problems and to share mathematical ideas and solutions. Six aspects (counting, measuring, locating, designing, explaining, and playing) are used regardless of where people live or what cultures they represent. Although people around the world use the same six functions, it is important that students come to understand that people approach these functions differently because of their culture. As students learn to use these six universal math skills, teachers can help them understand the interrelatedness of culture and its relationship to math. To do this, teachers need a broad understanding of mathematical concepts and knowledge of how these skills are used globally.

The National Council of Teachers of Mathematics (2000) advocates that teachers consider the following as they incorporate a global perspective into these six universal math skills:

- How students' linguistic, ethnic, racial, gender, and socioeconomic backgrounds influence their learning of mathematics
- The role of mathematics in society and culture, the contribution of various cultures to the advancement of mathematics, and the relationship of school mathematics to other subjects and realistic applications

Counting

The ability to count is a basic mathematical skill, and many students have learned to count before entering school. While they can do the basic skills of counting objects and items, most students lack a basic understanding of the concepts behind why and how they count. A study of these concepts can be used to help students understand that while counting is a universal skill, cultures determine how quantities are counted by naming certain amounts of objects with words or symbols.

Most cultures count in groups of ten. Zaslavsky (2004) states that the reason for this is simple—we have ten fingers. Therefore, base ten is and has been used throughout most cultures of the world as the basis of counting for more than 5,000 years; the early Egyptians, for example, were using a system of written numerals based on grouping by tens. On the other hand, the peoples of West Africa and Middle America, as well as the Inuit of the far north, group by twenties. In some languages, such as Mende of Sierra Leone, the word for twenty means "a whole person"—all the fingers and toes. The Mayan Math website contains information on using the Mayan system of base twenty in the classroom.

Trade books on counting provide a cultural view of how children count around the world. *Can You Count Ten Toes?* by Lezlie Evans is a trade book that teaches children to learn to count to ten in ten different languages, using the familiar counting structure as a springboard to sample languages from each continent. The Willesden Bookshop website contains a listing of hundreds of multicultural counting books. A unit using multicultural trade books in math is available at Counting Around the World.

The African board game of Oware is a counting game that requires counting seeds visually and remembering where certain numbers of seeds are located. Oware is one of the oldest existing board games in the world. It belongs to the pit-and-pebbles classification of games, which has been around for more than 5,000 years. Learning the game not only develops mathematical skills but teaches African traditions as well. An interactive version of the game is available at the Oware website. Sofweb provides links to eleven additional counting games from around the world.

For more advanced students, a study of base ten can be done through Chinese stick math. Developed by the Chinese more than 2,000 years ago, stick math is a quick and efficient way to deal with calculations required by commerce—buying, selling, counting quantities, and deducting payments. As the name suggests, numbers are shaped with sticks on a counting board. The board and sticks together make up a system for manipulating numbers—a precursor of the abacus and a kind of manual calculator. This game can be found at the Chinese Stick Math website and offers a view of math outside Western traditions and a perspective different from standard classroom learning experiences.

Measuring

People assign value or dimension to objects. These values are known as standard measurement and are used for time, weight, and distance.

Many of these standard measurements are universal and used around the world. Others are specific to a country or region.

The United States has been unique as one of the few countries in the world not using the metric system. As the U.S. population has become more mobile and more dependent on relationships with the rest of the world, the need for a one-world form of measurement has become more evident. It is argued that not using the metric system limits communication of scientific discoveries and economic issues and between world markets. For these reasons, the U.S. Congress passed the Metric Conversion Act of 1975 to promote the use of the metric system. Unfortunately, citizens rejected this conversion, and thirty years later, the English system of measurement is still the standard in the United States.

In March of 2000, the National Council of Teachers of Mathematics created a policy recommending the use of the metric system as the primary measurement system in mathematics instruction. It stressed that at an international level, the metric system is the standard system of measurement in the scientific and industrial worlds. In order for students to compete in a world that already functions with this system, students need to be competent with the metric system. This policy advocates not the abandonment of the English system but rather the understanding that the metric system is the measurement used in the majority of the world. Students must also learn the process of conversion if they are become competent in a global society.

Lesson plans abound on the Internet that teach not only the conversion process but also the history of the metric system. The U.S. Metric Association provides tips for teaching about the metric system, and at DiscoverySchool.com, teachers will find a unit, The Metric World, that can be adapted for many grade levels.

The study of the measurement of time is another element of standard measurement. For example, students can discover different aspects of the ancient Egyptian calendar system, and teachers can find lessons plans for teaching how to tell time and understanding the world time zones at Time for Time.

Measurement is necessary to determine the width, length, and perimeter of objects. Students can learn how to measure perimeter and area while learning about other cultures. A great website is The Aztec:

Markets, Maize, and Mathematics, where students learn not only how to measure perimeter and area but also about Aztec culture. Arizona State University has developed a wonderful interactive website called Hispanic Math, where students can learn about perimeter and area. The video is available in English and Spanish and allows students to learn how to measure in a fun, interactive way.

Some measurements are nonstandard, such as using parts of the body for units of measurement. Examples of nonstandard measuring might be 1) using the hands to measure the height of horses; 2) using the forearm as a measuring tool, as in the ancient "cubit"; or 3) measuring cloth and other objects from the nose to the end of the middle finger when the arm is outstretched, as the Shoshoni Native Americans traditionally did.

Locating

From sextants used by ancient sailors to modern global positioning systems, math has been used to help people determine direction, distance, and location. There are hundreds of ways to help students see the connection between math and location. Many of these ideas also help students learn about other cultures as they learn to find distance and location. Lesson plans and interactive activities to teach about location include the following:

- A unit for teaching global positioning systems.
- A lesson plan that allows students to observe the patterns of day and night visually utilizing a satellite image of the earth in real time and to learn about latitude and longitude.
- A classroom exercise called Global Positioning System Classroom Exercise: Where Am I?, which helps students understand the concept of triangulation.
- An interactive lesson plan called The Stowaway Adventure, which allows students to find locations around the world. This lesson provides an exciting way for students to gain an understanding of the motion of objects and how the speed and direction of an object are calculated using mathematics, introduces students to the use of real-time real-world data from the Internet, and allows students to apply traditional mathematics and science concepts to a real-world problem.

Designing

Many cultural designs are based on mathematical principles. This intersection of ideas and mathematics can be expressed through patterns, colors, or other physical materials. Cultural designs are found in buildings, paintings, weaving, hook art, crafts, mosaics, and drawings and are used to convey beauty, appreciation, self-expression, and heritage.

Geometry can be found in many of these cultural designs even though those creating the designs lacked a basic knowledge of geometry. The design often involves repeated patterns that have been passed from generation to generation. Tessellations are patterns developed by arranging repeated shapes in a mosaic pattern. Tessellations are found around the world and can be used to teach about the people and culture of a country. The Mathforum website has an excellent activity that provides information about tessellations and tilings from around the world.

Repeated patterns and designs are often used as a means of protection. Rangavalli patterns are found in many parts of India. These are patterns created early in the morning on the front step of the home that help protect the home from evil luck. The patterns are made with grains trailed on the floor from the open hand. Patterns and designs such as these and other multicultural math ideas can be found at the Multicultural Mathematics website.

Explaining

Visual representations are used to communicate various ideas, concepts, and data. Mathematical concepts are explained through graphic organizers, bar and line graphs, charts, and Venn diagrams. The National Council of Teachers of Mathematics has two standards, communications and representation, that directly relate to the issue of using mathematics to explain and describe. Under the communications standard, the objectives state that students are to do the following:

- Organize and consolidate their mathematical thinking though communication
- Communicate their mathematical thinking coherently and clearly to peers, teachers, and others

- Analyze and evaluate the mathematical thinking and strategies of others
- Use the language of mathematics to express mathematical ideas precisely

The representation standard suggests that students must be able to do the following:

- Create and use representations to organize, record, and communicate mathematical ideas
- Select, apply, and translate among mathematical representations to solve problems
- Use representations to model and interpret physical, social, and mathematical phenomena (National Council of Teachers of Mathematics, 2000)

The Illuminations website of the National Council of Teachers of Mathematics provides hundreds of lesson plans that promote the use of mathematics as a communication tool. An example of such a lesson involves determining the world density concentration. In this lesson, students research the populations of five different countries. They then plot the information they found in graph form and present their findings to the class. This activity allows for research on different countries and for students to learn how to present this information in a format that explains mathematical data.

Playing

Piaget (1962) noted that play is a natural and inherent characteristic of individuals across cultures, asserting that children respond spontaneously to gamelike activities. Through play and games, children expand their understanding of themselves and others, their knowledge of the world and various cultures, and their ability to communicate with peers and adults. Games and play are viewed as vehicles for knowledge and skill development and attitude formation.

Mathematical games can foster mathematical communication as students explain and justify their moves to one another. In addition, games can motivate students and engage them in thinking about and applying concepts and skills. Through mathematical games, opportunities are created that allow students to construct their own understanding of a specific mathematical concept and/or skill. Games involve so many mathematical skills and strategies that gaming participation can be considered a universal mathematical activity. In 1989, even the National Council of Teachers of Mathematics stated that most of its standards for teaching mathematics were incorporated in games, specifically estimation, probability, and operations (Barta & Schaelling, 1999).

There are many international games with a mathematical design. These games promote not only mathematical skills but also cultural awareness and global understanding. The trade books *International Games* by Valjean McLenighan and *Math Games and Activities from Around the World* by Claudia Zaslavsky give many examples of games from other cultures that require mathematical skills. The Internet is another source for hundreds of math games that provide global awareness. Examples of multicultural math games available on the Internet are the following:

- Tangram is a centuries-old Chinese tile game consisting of seven geometric shapes. Students can learn its history and create their own games at the Tangrams website.
- The Mankala family of games is among the oldest of human entertainments and has been played for generations around the world. They are played on a board with fourteen pits that are scooped out or simply drawn on the ground. Online play occurs at the Mankala website.
- The game of Konane is a game that was played in ancient Hawaii. It was played on huge stones called "papamu." There are small impressions, or "puka," in the "papamu," or playing board, where the playing pieces were placed. In old Hawaii, the original game pieces that were used were black and white pebbles. Dark and light seashells were also used.
- The Tower of Hanoi puzzle was invented by the French mathematician Edouard Lucas in 1883. The objective is to transfer the entire tower from one peg to one of the other pegs, moving only one disk at a time and never a larger one onto a smaller. The puzzle is well known to upper-level math students since it appears in virtually any introductory text on data structures or algorithms.

MATH WORD PROBLEMS

Mathematical word problems present an excellent opportunity to enhance global awareness. Often there is a disconnect between culture
and mathematics, especially in word problems. Since mathematical
word problems are typically formed around students' family lives and
experiences, students' backgrounds and cultures define the meaning of
the teacher's wording of the problems.

In divergent cultures, there can be differences in meanings for the
same problems. For example, students might display a lack of interest,
confusion, or even inadequate cognitive understanding when a word
problem contains calculations of how many ornaments are to be pur-
chased for the Christmas tree, counting how many days to a holiday, or
other word problems centered around any particular holiday that some
cultures do not observe or celebrate. It's apparent that if the student is
somehow disconnected from the word problems because of a lack of
interest or no understanding of the content, solving the problems will
certainly not occur. Word problems cannot be developed in cultural iso-
lation; there must be consideration of the students' background knowledge in problem construction.

Keeping in mind the challenge of clarity in cross-cultural communication when teaching mathematics, word problems can be structured as
an instrument for social changes and for awareness of global problems.
By structuring the wording of the problems to reflect such broad social
issues as world trade, the spread and control of disease, global economics, occupations as defined by gender, and financial interdependence, students develop math skills and global perspectives.

MULTIDISCIPLINARY APPROACH TO GLOBAL ISSUES

Multicultural mathematics education should include meaningful math
activities integrated with other subjects. This requires joint planning
with teachers from other disciplines. This multidisciplinary approach
helps students understand the relevance of mathematics to social studies, language arts, science, and related arts.

Math teachers can support the activities of their fellow teachers by
using topics discussed in other classes as examples and problems when

teaching the math curriculum. This does not require a change from the planned curriculum. Instead, students can measure distance, compute the exchange of money, and use information about a country studied in social studies. An example can be found at the website Geometry from the Land of the Incas, which provides many ways that Inca culture can be viewed from a geometric point of view.

Teachers from various disciplines can work together to focus on a particular country, region, or culture. At China Online, teachers will find a five-day interdisciplinary unit that provides students an understanding of Chinese customs, history, geography, and educational practices and an opportunity to compare and contrast their findings. Students publish or share their findings using technology and traditional methods. These multidisciplinary activities deepen a student's understanding of the topic studied.

THE VALUE OF MULTICULTURAL MATHEMATICS

Just as literacy has come to mean more than reading and writing, mathematics must also be thought as more than just counting, calculating, sorting, and comparing. It must be viewed as a way to prepare students for a new age of mathematically based technology and unprecedented means of communication (D'Ambrosio, 2001). Teachers must help students develop mathematical skills that will prepare them to participate and be successful in the twenty-first century.

As classrooms become more diverse, teachers can use innovative and useful ways to teach mathematics by embracing the concept of global education. This is an excellent way to explore mathematics so that students can not only better understand and learn concepts, but also appreciate and experience the ways mathematics is used by different cultures. The positive aspects of providing a global perspective to the teaching of mathematics are the following:

- Students have their cultural dignity reaffirmed and restored.
- Students come to understand how mathematics continues to be culturally adapted and used by people around the world.
- Students come to understand that they are mathematically capable.

- Students come to understand that they possess a long and rich mathematical heritage.
- Students become aware of the role of mathematics in all societies. They realize that mathematical practices arose out of people's real needs and interests.
- Students learn to appreciate the contributions of cultures different from their own and to take pride in their own heritage.
- Students come to understand the linkage of the study of mathematics with history, language arts, fine arts, and other subjects; all the disciplines take on more meaning.
- Students of all backgrounds see their cultural heritage in the subject area, and this builds their self-esteem and interest in mathematics.
- Students see their teachers as role models in how they should value diversity in the classroom and in the world.
- Students develop critical thinking skills and the ability to work cooperatively.
- Students learn to solve mathematical problems by applying multiple strategies and ideas.

D'Ambrosio (2001) states, "Mathematics is a compilation of progressive discoveries and inventions from cultures around the world during the course of history. Its history and ethnography form a wonderful mosaic of cultural contributions" (online). Through the marriage of global education and mathematics, students become part of this mosaic.

INSTRUCTIONAL IDEAS

Integrating Math and Multimedia Presentations

The Global Economy: The World Monetary System is an activity designed for students in grades 9 to 12 and focuses on foreign currency exchange in the global economy. While some students may realize that foreign currency exchange rates affect the international traveler, few understand the direct effects that these rates have on people who may never leave their communities. This lesson is designed to make students aware of international monetary transactions and to show them how the jobs they hold and the purchases they make in their local community are affected by the foreign currency exchange market.

The lesson consists of four detailed exercises dealing with currency exchange rates, currency equivalents and changing money, results of the Asian economic crisis, and changes in the value of the dollar. An additional suggested activity is to ask students to start out in a different country and plan a major trip to another country very distant from them. They estimate the cost of such a trip given the value of the currency on any one day. Various travel websites can be incorporated to help students find the necessary information. Students then present the information to their classmates in a multimedia format such as a PowerPoint presentation or a Web page.

Integrating Math and Telecomputing Projects

Participants in the Angle of the Sun project measure how high the sun is above the horizon and then submit their findings to a database. They then look at the data reported by other students to identify patterns. The purpose of this activity is to allow students to practice measuring, communicating, and collaborating with others on a research project, analyzing data, and drawing possible conclusions from or about any patterns they discover.

Students calculate the angle of the sun above the horizon by measuring the shadow of a meter stick. They submit their findings along with other geographic and meteorological information to a Web page database that can then be viewed, graphed, and analyzed to look for patterns around the world. While participating in this project, students engage in deductive reasoning, problem solving, and critical thinking as they communicate with other students globally. Additionally, they learn about the sun, its motions through the sky, and how this affects us.

Integrating Math and Online Discussions

Down the Drain: How Much Water Do You Use? is a multidisciplinary collaborative project that allows students to share information about water usage with other students from around the country and the world. Based on data collected by their household members and their classmates, students determine the average amount of water used by one person in a day. They compare this to the average amount of water used per person per day in other parts of the world.

This project, appropriate for students in grades 4 to 8, integrates math and science as students take part in collecting, measuring, and reporting the average amount of water their class uses each day. The data must be reported in gallons and liters so that students have an opportunity to make those conversions and discuss the advantages and disadvantages of using the metric system. The data from all participating schools are compiled in a spreadsheet and used to summarize typical water usage around the world. Links to a student area and a teacher area allow participants to share their results, photos, and information about themselves and the project with other participants. The site also includes an Ask an Expert section with links to the e-mail addresses of water, math, and science specialists.

Integrating Math and Web-Based Lessons

Melting Pot Math is an activity from Philadelphia's Franklin Institute online resources. Students solve math problems inspired by cultures from around the world. This collection of more than fifty sets of problems from ten areas of the world offers challenging problems that help students see the connections between math and the world.

Each set of problems begins with a short description, including any necessary numerical information, about an important cultural aspect from the selected area of the world. Following the description are six to eight word problems that students can solve using the information and data provided in the description. Students in grades 4 to 8 can practice a wide variety of practical math skills as they learn more about the world they share with others.

An example of this activity can be found in the set of problems about monsoons in India. Students are provided with information about the impact of monsoons on India's climate as well as tables with rainfall and high temperature data. They then use the given information to solve problems and construct graphs based on the average rainfall and range of temperature for different Indian cities.

INTERNET RESOURCES

Ancient Egypt Calendar System: http://www.mnsu.edu/emuseum/prehistory/
egypt/dailylife/calendar.html

Angle of the Sun: http://www.waukesha.k12.wi.us/South/EarthScience/
AngleOfTheSun/AngleOfTheSun.shtml

The Aztec: Markets, Maize, and Mathematics: http://www.mts.net/~lsisco/
PAGE4.HTM

China Online: http://etc.sccoe.org/i2000/china1.htm

Chinese Stick Math: http://www.enc.org/features/focus/archive/mathroots2/
document.shtm?input=FOC-003612-index

Counting Around the World: http://www.uen.org/Lessonplan/preview.cgi?
LPid=5706

Down the Drain: How Much Water Do You Use?: http://www.ciese.org/
curriculum/drainproj/

Geometry from the Land of the Incas: http://agutie.homestead.com/files/
index.html

The Global Economy: The World Monetary System: http://www.globaled.org/
curriculum/money.html

Global Positioning System Classroom Exercise: Where Am I?: http://octopus
.gma.org/space1/where.html

Global Positioning Systems: http://web.haystack.mit.edu/pcr/whereami/
gps.htm

Hispanic Math: http://tblr.ed.asu.edu/hmp/hmp_beta.html

Illuminations: http://illuminations.nctm.org/index.asp

Konane: http://www.k12.hi.us/~gkaapuni/konane.htm

Latitude and Longitude: http://education.ssc.nasa.gov/fad/detail.asp?Lesson
ID=23

Mankala: http://www.elf.org/mankala/Mankala.html

Mathforum: http://mathforum.org/sum95/suzanne/historytess.html

Mayan Math: http://www.hanksville.org/yucatan/mayamath.html

Multicultural Mathematics: http://www.cyffredin.co.uk/

Oware: http://www.oware.clara.net/page2.html

Sofweb: http://www.sofweb.vic.edu.au/litnumweek/eys/games/multicultural/
counting.htm

The Stowaway Adventure: http://www.k12science.org/curriculum/shipproj/

Tangrams: http://tangrams.ca/

Time for Time: http://www.time-for-time.com/zonesworld.htm

Tower of Hanoi: http://www.cut-the-knot.org/recurrence/hanoi.shtml

U.S. Metric Association: http://lamar.colostate.edu/~hillger/week.htm

Willesden Bookshop: http://www.willesdenbookshop.co.uk/index.htm

REFERENCES

Barta, J., & Schaelling, D. (1999). Games we play: Connecting mathematics and culture in the classroom. *Teaching Children Mathematics*, *4*, 388–393.

Chronicle of Higher Education. (October 6, 2000). *Colloquy*. Retrieved from http://chronicle.com/colloquy/2000/ethnomath/ethnomath.htm

D'Ambrosio, U. (2001). What is ethnomathematics, and how can it help children in schools? *Teaching Children Mathematics*, *7*, 308–310.

Mathematics makes a world of difference in our lives! (2001). *Teaching Children Mathematics*, *7*, 344.

National Council of Teachers of Mathematics. (2000). *Principles and standards for school mathematics*. Reston, VA: NCTM. http://www.nctm.org

Piaget, J. (1962). *Play, dreams, and imitation in childhood*. New York: Norton.

Spring, J. (2000). *The intersection of cultures*. Boston: McGraw-Hill.

Zaslavsky, C. (2004). *World cultures in the mathematics class*. Retrieved from http://www.enc.org/features/focus/archive/multi/document.shtm?input=AC Q-111364-1364

CHAPTER 9

Global Education and Literature

Children are the world's most valuable resource and its best hope
for the future.

—John F. Kennedy, former president of United States,
UNICEF appeal, July 25, 1963

Language arts teachers have long understood the power of children's
literature to influence students' lives. Literature goes beyond merely
providing content to acting as a powerful stimulus to trigger emotions
and feelings. Children's literature provides a means for students to
understand their own wants and needs, but more important, it provides a way for students to learn that children around the world have
the same wants and needs. It allows students to see the commonalities of emotions, commitments, dreams, and expectations they have
with the world beyond their communities. For these reasons, children's literature is an important vehicle for providing a global perspective to the curriculum.

Language arts teachers realize the importance of integrating the language processes of reading, writing, speaking, and listening with culture and content. The two major national organizations for language
arts teachers, the International Reading Association and the National
Council of Teachers of English, have included language in their standards to emphasize that learning about others and their culture is an important aspect of the language arts curriculum. Their national standards
recommend the following:

- Students read a wide range of print and nonprint texts to build an understanding of texts, of themselves, and of the cultures of the United States and the world; to acquire new information; to respond to the needs and demands of society and the workplace; and for personal fulfillment. Among these texts are fiction and nonfiction, classic and contemporary works.
- Students read a wide range of literature from many periods in many genres to build an understanding of the many dimensions (such as philosophical, ethical, and aesthetic) of human experience.
- Students develop an understanding of and respect for diversity in language use, patterns, and dialects across cultures, ethnic groups, geographic regions, and social roles (International Reading Association, 1996).

A study of literature through high-quality children's books facilitates these standards. The visual appeal of the illustrations found in children's books encourages students to learn more regarding people that differ from them. Literature can expose students to new ideas and different people in a powerful way. Children's literature is available for students of all ages and includes picture books, traditional tales and fantasy, poetry, realistic and historical fiction, biography, and informational and multicultural books. Each of these types of books can be a bridge to another culture.

Quality literature increases student awareness and understanding of cultural concepts. Norton (1990) lists several additional benefits for students when reading and discussing carefully selected cultural literature for global study. Cultural literature study enables students to do the following:

- Develop an awareness of diverse backgrounds and an appreciation of a literary heritage
- Learn to feel empathy with people who are represented in the texts
- Discover the folktales, legend, myths, and fables that represent the values and beliefs of the people
- Discover the stories of the past on which cultures are founded
- Discover the themes and values that are woven chronologically from the past to the present and continue in importance to the culture

LITERACY CURRICULUM ORGANIZATION FOR GLOBAL STUDY

The idea of how best to integrate a global literacy curriculum into the total schooling of students is not a new concern. A global emphasis can be presented at every age and grade level as long as the teacher is cognizant of the developmental maturity level of the students.

Early Grades (Pre-K–2)

In the early childhood stage (grades pre-K–2), global study should be directed primarily toward cultural relations between individuals and is designed to increase the students' oral language development. Students in this age-group have extremely short attention spans, are emotionally vulnerable, and are egocentric. Global study, therefore, should be focused on students' interests and the familiar. In preschool and kindergarten classrooms, global education focuses on a comparative study of families at home and around the globe. By widening the curriculum throughout the world, children gain a global perspective. In this way, the early childhood teacher plays an important part in laying a foundation for young children's sense of world citizenship.

Multicultural books provide a bridge from the known to the unknown when the teacher introduces a new concept about a person or culture. The students' own culture is familiar and aids in crossing the cultural gaps for children in both preoperational stages to concrete, operational stages. For this grade level, trade books used to teach about the world should develop global awareness and engage emotional responses in children and use something common and well-known to the student as a link to other cultures (Lickteig & Danielson, 1995).

Students at this age level need to realize that children around the world have families, live in some type of home, and play games. Simple books focusing on one theme are useful to promote this concept. At The Willesden Bookshop, teachers will find a listing of such simple books. At this website, teachers will find books that teach about families, clothes, toys, and shoes from a global perspective and show that these are common elements in every culture. All are topics to which students relate on a very personal level.

Two additional books help pre-K–2 students make a connection to the world beyond their community. *All Kinds of People* by Emma Damon is a simple lift-the-flap book that introduces young children to the concept of diversity in a humorous fashion. Comic pictures, with flaps, foldout pages, and cutouts, emphasize that all people are special and are characterized by an infinite variety of shapes, sizes, skin tones, hairstyles, interests, and hobbies.

Hello World! Greetings in 42 Languages around the Globe by Stojic Manya provides students a sampler of the world's languages. Full-page color pictures of children's faces—with varied shapes and skin tones appropriate to its international cast—include colored bands with captions in enlarged text showing the word for "hello" in each language, with a phonetic equivalent printed underneath. The fun of learning languages can be expanded at the Kidspace, where students can hear the word "hello" spoken in more than twenty languages. Students in the lower grades will enjoy practicing their greetings in the world's languages.

Upper Elementary Grades (Grades 3–5)

In the upper elementary grades (grades 3–5), increased independent work that calls for inquiry techniques of critical reading is added to developing literacy skills. Students at this age comprehend broader concepts and can deal with issues of diversity, tolerance, justice, prejudice, and acceptance. During these years, students are particularly open to knowledge regarding other cultures and worldviews. Discussions of issues of acceptance are important because students become more ethnocentric during the middle years. It is important that younger students come to understand that humans share more commonalities than differences and that, in situations in which similarities cause conflict, acceptance and tolerance are needed.

Two books that help students see that people around the world share common needs and desires are *Children Just Like Me* and *Children Just Like Me: Celebrations!* by Kindersley and Kindersley. To create this remarkable book, a photographer and a teacher traveled to more than thirty countries, meeting and interviewing children. Each child's story is recorded in these books, published to coincide with the fiftieth anniversary of the United Nations Children's Fund (UNICEF). Extraordinary photographs bring to life the children's families and homes, their clothes and food, their friends and favorite games, and other aspects of their daily lives. Each child presented has hopes and fears, dreams and beliefs. Their cultures are different, yet in many ways their daily lives are very similar, as are their hopes for the future and their ways of looking at the world.

These books can be used in a variety of ways. One interesting lesson plan, Multiculturalism and Me-Lesson Plan Incorporating a Database, involves teaching students how to create a database and a spreadsheet by using Just Like Me as a springboard for discussion. At Crossroad of Cultures, teachers will find lesson plans to support Just Like Me and links for investigation of the countries highlighted in the book.

Middle School

Middle school students tend to be very self-oriented as they begin the trials of adolescence. It is a time for students to expand and explore their degree of knowledge, self-awareness, and self-expression. Therefore, it is beneficial for educators to use fiction and nonfiction that allows the students to better understand their own struggles and to see that students from the other parts of the world have similar struggles. The Middle School Book List provides age-appropriate books that are classics, historical fiction, modern fiction, biographies, dramas, and science and fantasy.

An ageless story that speaks to the struggles of adolescence and an understanding how people treat and mistreat others is "Anne Frank: The Diary of a Young Girl." The Web English Teacher site provides numerous links to lesson plans and activities to accompany the reading of this book. At the Anne Frank Museum website, students can participate in a virtual field trip to Anne Frank's hiding place. This site also provides outstanding lesson ideas and teaching materials.

Carol Bierman's book *Journey to Ellis Island: How My Father Came to America* is the personal story of the immigration of her father and her family from Russia through Ellis Island. Because immigration concerns are such a current topic with community interest, further research and real-life projects could result from this book study. An excellent unit using this book as the foundation of study can be found at Ellis Island: Gateway to America. Through several activities, students learn that immigrants arriving at Ellis Island came from different countries and for different reasons. The lesson plan includes a variety of instructional media, including the use of video clips and websites. Another excellent online resource to use in conjunction with this book is Scholastic's Interactive Tour of Ellis Island.

High School

Students in grades 9 to 12 can expand their skills, abilities, and literacy knowledge into courses of action by analyzing cultural, social, economic, and political systems presented through high-quality fiction. Fiction offers high school students a way to confront and discuss difficult issues in a respectful way. Novels can reveal to students an existence very different from their own while offering them a safe distance from which to discuss their feelings, prejudices, and experience with racism and people of different races.

In her work with high school students, Bender-Slack (2002) found that they care deeply about human injustices and enjoy books that give a voice to their concerns. Global injustice can be discussed through books that chronicle the horrors of war. Dennis Bock's *The Ash Garden* allows students to discuss the issue of nuclear warfare from three different perspectives. Such a book can be a springboard for further research into the issues of power, peace, and war.

Several Internet sites provide a listing of outstanding multicultural books written for the grades 9 to 12. Exceptional lists are found at the following sites:

- Multicultural Literature for Adolescents
- The Alan Review
- Booklists for Young Adults on the Web

Regardless of age level, teachers can use literature to help students learn about other cultures. Norton (1990) suggests that the use of literature should proceed from broader generalizations to specific cultural elements. The approach begins with using traditional literature to study a cultural group by including a broad array of folktales, myths, legends, and fables. The study can then be narrowed to the study of traditional tales from a few tribal or cultural areas. A study of a culture's history is then completed through cultural autobiographies, biographies, samples of expository texts, and historical cultural fiction. Finally, the study ends with current authentic fiction, poetry, and biographies reflective of the culture.

This sequential progression of instruction presents a global view of the culture from reading the different genres and great works of a particular culture. Because the cultural elements are presented in a sequential, interrelated manner, students gain increased personal understanding, an aesthetic appreciation and respect for the culture's artistic contributions, and improved sensitivity to other cultures. Such depths of understanding are unlikely with a one-shot approach to culture study.

A MULTIDISCIPLINARY APPROACH

Trade books play a unique role in helping students realize that they are members of a global community and, therefore, share in responsibilities for all humankind. Multicultural trade books can be easily integrated across the content areas of mathematics, science, social studies, and possibly physical education, art, music, and advisory times. The power of using trade books in a multidisciplinary approach is in the intensity of repetition throughout the day or weeks and in the experience of learning in various contexts within the content areas. Students come to realize that knowledge is not confined to one area as an isolated unit but rather relates to many situations and various contexts. Thematic use makes the integration and transfer of learning concepts easier and more meaningful.

For a multidisciplinary approach to be effective, literature teachers should collaborate with teachers in other content areas to identify academic, cross-curricular course work and global cultural activities that complement each other. Therefore, it is important for the language arts teachers to promote global education by finding appropriate and authentic children's and adolescent's literature to support instruction in the content areas.

Multicultural trade books supplement course texts in a variety of ways. Literature provides memorable contexts for the language. Text is much easier to reproduce, understand, and recall if it is structured episodically. Literature uses characters and plot so that students are engaged cognitively and emotionally. Moss (1991) lists five distinct advantages of using trade books as an accompaniment to content area texts:

1. Trade books can be chosen to match the variety of reading levels of the students within the classroom. Often, content texts are written above the grade level for which the book was intended.
2. Trade books often are beautifully illustrated, assisting students in their visualization of the content.
3. Trade books enable students to pursue a topic of their interest more in depth. This wider reading allows students to have a broader view of a culture than an informational textbook.
4. Trade books are organized in a logical pattern that students can follow easily. Familiar story structures such as cause and effect, setting–problem–solution, or compare–contrast are easier for students to comprehend than a listing of facts, as textbooks sometimes contain.
5. Trade books stay current as new books are published each year, and the paperback editions are very inexpensive, while textbooks are costly and published every five to ten years.

Textbooks give students dates and facts; literature goes beyond knowledge into the internal realms of thinking and feeling. Through good-quality children's literature, students can "make a friend" from another culture or time. This "friendship" becomes the basis for understanding what is taught in the content areas and leads to connections to the world beyond the student's immediate community.

An example of how a trade book can be used in a multidisciplinary approach is the use of *Animal Dreaming* by Paul Morin. This is an Australian story of a young boy's first "walkabout" in the outback as part of a rite of passage. The use of this book can supplement a study of Australian history, geography, and science. The following are ideas for multidisciplinary integration:

- An art unit utilizing this book with the teaching of aboriginal art and technology can be found at Bark Painting Web page.

- A multidisciplinary unit focuses on geography, history, social studies, and science and incorporates the book *Animal Dreaming*.
- A unit for third graders, Aboriginal Dreamtime, is based on this book.

CRITERIA FOR BOOK SELECTION

Whether the literature teacher is selecting a trade book as part of the language arts curriculum or to supplement instruction provided in the other subject areas, book selection for classroom use is extremely important. An outstanding multicultural trade book is defined by the following criteria:

- The book illustrates and describes a variety of human characteristics in a culture, such as different occupations, different socioeconomic levels, and varying abilities and ambitions of its people.
- The book is free of subtle messages hidden within the context of the stories or materials that project a nationalistic viewpoint rather than a global perspective.
- The book avoids negative cultural stereotypes by focusing on similarities rather than differences and avoiding "us" versus "them" polarity.
- The book supports the teacher's instruction of a diverse culture in a global curriculum. The book should enhance the planned objectives and outcomes of the global activity and reflect an authentic view of the culture being studied.
- The book should be rich in cultural details, honoring and celebrating diversity as well as common bonds in humanity.
- The book should use authentic names for characters, represent both positive and negative behaviors and traits, and accurately portray gender role.
- The book is written from the perspective of someone who lives in a particular region or country and not from an American perspective.

Nonfiction trade books are evaluated annually for classroom use by respected content organizations in many subject areas. The National Science Teachers Association publishes a listing of notable trade books each year in their Outstanding Science Trade Books for Children. The

National Council for the Social Studies also publishes a listing of recommended books on its website. The Notable Books for Global Society compiled by the International Reading Association provides an annual list of outstanding trade books for enhancing student understanding of people and cultures throughout the world.

ONE BOOK, MANY CULTURES

The interpretation of literature varies from culture to culture, both linguistically and cognitively. The comparison of a familiar story told from the perspectives of diverse cultures is a way for teachers to introduce a global perspective to the classroom. A story often used by teachers for this purpose is the ageless story of Cinderella. The Cinderella story can be found in many countries and in many cultures and is an example of how the same story can be told in a variety of ways depending on the culture's boundaries from which it is presented. Table 9.1 provides a listing of books from a variety of countries and cultures in which the Cinderella story is the theme.

From kindergarten to college classrooms, Cinderella projects, book clubs, and WebQuests are used to study the story's appeal and varied cultural history to demonstrate how different cultures deal with the same theme. Lesson plans focus on identifying commonalities and dif-

Table 9.1   Cinderella Stories from Around the World.

Cinderella by Charles Perrault (traditional European story)
Abadeha: The Philippine Cinderella by Myma J. de la Paz
Adelita: A Mexican Cinderella Story by Tomie dePaola
Angkat: The Cambodian Cinderella by Jewell Reinhart Coburn
Cendrillon: A Caribbean Cinderella by Robert D. San Souci
Domitila: A Cinderella Tale from the Mexican Tradition by Jewell Reinhart Coburn and
    Connie McLennan
Egyptian Cinderella by Shirley Climo
Fair, Brown and Trembling by Jude Daly (Irish story)
Golden Sandal: Middle Eastern Cinderella Story by Rebecca Hickox
Jouanah: a Hmong Cinderella by Jewell Reinhart and Tzexa Lee
Korean Cinderella by Shirley Climo
Little Gold Star/Estrellita de Oro by Joe Hayes (Hispanic version)
Rough-Face Girl by Rafe Martin and David Shannon (Native American version)
Vasilissa the Beautiful: A Russian Folktale by Elizabeth Winthrop
Way Meat Loves Salt: A Jewish Cinderella by Nina Jaffe
Yeh-Shen: A Cinderella Story from China by Ai-Ling Louie

ferences in plot and helping students understand the universal appeal of the Cinderella story. The Cinderella story can be used in a multidisciplinary unit with lessons available for social studies, mathematics, geography, art, and technology. An Internet search for lesson plans on the Cinderella story produces hundreds of lesson plans. Three of the most useful sites are the following:

- Children's Literature: Lesson Plans and Resources
- The "Cinderella" Story
- Teacher Resources

CONCLUSION

By providing class time for reading appropriate children's and adolescent's literature for global study, students can develop lifetime reading habits and learn to become active and productive world citizens. When students use their literacy skills of reading and writing to participate in a global study, they make a connection between their personal feelings and attitudes and their respect and understanding of those from other cultures. Cultural literacy study with a global focus should result in students who value themselves as individuals and members of the world community, who appreciate the similarities more than differences within people, and who desire to eliminate the causes of stereotypes, prejudice, and discrimination in the world.

INSTRUCTIONAL IDEAS

Integrating Reading/Language Arts and Web-Based Lessons

Etymologic is an online interactive game that challenges students to correctly identify the cultural origin of commonly used words in the English language. In this etymology game, players are presented with ten randomly selected etymology (word origin) or word definition puzzles to solve. In each case, the word or phrase is highlighted in bold, and several possible answers are given. Students try to choose the correct answer to score a point for that question. False answers often seem quite plausible, and some of the true answers are hard to believe, but all answers are documented.

This interactive game is appropriate for independent play by middle and high school students or as a whole-class or small-group activity for younger students. Getting the right answer can be quite difficult, but correct answers and explanations of the origins are given after each try. Discovering the true origin for commonly used vocabulary words can be a culturally enriching activity for students and adults of all ages.

Integrating Reading/Language Arts and Online Discussions

Reader's Theater is a language arts activity in which students tell a story by reading directly from a script without props, costumes, or sets. Actors do not memorize lines but are familiar enough with the script that they can add inflection and motions appropriate to their characters' words. Although reader's theater was first used as a way to introduce literature in a theatrical form at the college level, it is now considered a successful instructional activity for students in lower grades. Reader's theater has been found effective not only for instruction in reading but also for social studies, as many of the scripts are often based on stories from other cultures.

As a former professional reader's theater actor and author of children's books, Aaron Shepard has written dozens of scripts based on multicultural folk stories from countries such as India, China, Iraq, Pakistan, Finland, and Tanzania and makes them available for students and teachers at his Reader's Theater website. Additionally, Shepard provides an online form for students to use to contact him with any questions they may have about the background of the stories and the scripts. This professional advice and feedback from an expert in the field will help students develop a deeper understanding of literature from other cultures.

Integrating Reading/Language Arts and Telecomputing Projects

Famous Stories Travel Around the World is an example on a telecomputing project that gives students the opportunity to get to know their own literature better as well as the literature of other countries. It also gives them a reason to try to write well and to provide a showcase for their finished work.

This project, sponsored by a seventh-grade class, collects stories for children written by famous writers from different countries. Participating students choose a story for children written by a well-known writer from their country, read it carefully, summarize it, and illustrate it. The students' summaries and scanned drawings or artworks are then published on the project Web page. By contributing to this project, participating students will have a part in enriching the world cultural heritage.

Integrating Reading/Language Arts and Multimedia Presentations

How are communities similar and different? Students can compare the characteristics of different communities using a Venn diagram created in a multimedia format. As a whole class activity, students brainstorm ideas to determine the essential components of a community. Then in small groups the students research the selected components of two communities from those described in the book *Children Just Like Me* by Kindersley and Kindersley.

Using drawing tools from a word-processing program, or a more specialized application such as *Kidspiration*, students create Venn diagrams comparing the two communities they chose to research. In the center section of the interlocking circles, students write or draw pictures of the components the two communities have in common. In the outer sections of the diagram, students place items that are different, so they can understand that these places have things in common despite their differences.

As a culminating activity, students present the diagrams to their classmates using presentation software. They can also post their diagrams to a class website to share with others.

INTERNET RESOURCES

Aboriginal Dreamtime: http://www2.milwaukee.k12.wi.us/multirc/pages/ Voices/pdfvoices/05dreamtime.pdf

The Alan Review: http://scholar.lib.vt.edu/ejournals/ALAN/fall95/Ericson.html

Animal Dreaming: http://www.naz.edu:9000/~alnicoli/Instructionalprojectl.html

Anne Frank Museum: http://www.annefrank.org/content.asp?pid=1&lid=2

Bark Painting: http://www.princetonol.com/groups/iad/lessons/elem/jan-aborig.htm

Booklists for Young Adults on the Web: http://www.seemore.mi.org/booklists/ fiction.html

Children's Literature: Lesson Plans and Resources: http://www.cloudnet.com/ ~edrbsass/edchildrenslit.htm#c

The "Cinderella" Story: http://www.webenglishteacher.com/cinderella.html

Crossroad of Cultures: http://www.texancultures.utsa.edu/crossroads/index6.htm

Ellis Island: Gateway to America: http://www.idahoptv.org/ntti/nttilessons/lessons2002/mittelstaedt.html

Famous Stories Travel Around the World: http://www.geocities.com/optionalcourse7a191/famous_stories_travel_around_the.htm

Interactive Tour of Ellis Island: http://teacher.scholastic.com/activities/immigration/tour/index.htm

Kidspace: http://www.ipl.org/div/kidspace/hello/

Kidspiration: http://www.inspiration.com/productinfo/kidspiration/index.cfm

Middle School Book List: http://www.ea1785.org/htm/AcadS/librarysystem/annenmiddle/readinglists/recreadinglist.html

Multicultural Literature for Adolescents: http://www.pampetty.com/multiadolescent.htm

Multiculturalism and Me-Lesson Plan Incorporating a Database: http://eduweb.brandonu.ca/~edtech/class/spread/multi-me.htm

National Council for the Social Studies: http://www.socialstudies.org/resources/notable/

Notable Books for Global Society: http://www.csulb.edu/org/childrens-lit/proj/nbgs/intro-nbgs.html

Outstanding Science Trade Books for Children: http://www.nsta.org/ostbc

Reader's Theater: http://www.aaronshep.com/rt/index.html

Teacher Resources: http://www.bernardsboe.com/Mount-Prospect/Library/Cinderella/Teachers.htm

Web English Teacher: http://www.webenglishteacher.com/frank.html

The Willesden Bookshop: http://www.willesdenbookshop.co.uk/index.htm

REFERENCES

Bender-Slack, D. (2002). Using literature to teach global education: A humanist approach. *English Journal, 91*, 70–75.

International Reading Association. (1996). *Standards for the English language arts*. Retrieved November 16, 2004, from http://www.reading.org/resources/issues/reports/learning_standards.html

Lickteig, M. J., & Danielson, K. E. (1995). Use children's books to link the cultures of the world. *Social Studies, 86*, 69–74.

Moss, B. (1991). Children's nonfiction trade books: A complement to content area texts. *The Reading Teacher, 45*, 26–31.

Norton, D. E. (1990). Teaching multicultural literature in the reading curriculum. *The Reading Teacher, 44*, 28–40.

CHAPTER 10

Global Awareness through the Related Arts

I am enough of an artist to draw freely upon my imagination. Imagination is more important than knowledge. Knowledge is limited. Imagination encircles the world.

—Albert Einstein, "What Life Means to Einstein: An Interview
by George Sylvester Viereck," for the Oct. 26, 1929,
issue of the *Saturday Evening Post*

Teachers realize that their instructional content and activities have a significant influence on students' early sensitivity, awareness, and understanding of global issues. It is becoming evident, however, that global consciousness should not be restricted to the confines of the four walls of a classroom or to the study of global issues in the content areas. Through related arts—physical education, art, music, and drama—students develop an understanding of world cultures, peoples, events, places, and issues. Instruction and activities in the related arts can help teachers convey positive global images and perspectives and demystify cultural stereotypes.

USING RELATED ARTS TO PROMOTE GLOBAL ISSUES

As early as 1964, Bereday and Lauwerys identified seven attributes that are developed or strengthened through organized games and sports. These same attributes are developed through music, art, and drama classes. Games, sports, art, music, and drama allow students to practice with the components of life itself—to try on roles and responsibilities within the safety of a classroom. These seven attributes closely relate to the five key cognitive and effective attributes associated with developing a global perspective identified by Case (1993). See Table 10.1 for a comparison of these two sets of attributes.

The seven attributes developed through the related arts and directly associated with developing a global perspective are the following:

Unselfishness: The acceptance of the common good as being of greater value than one's immediate interest, sociability, and willingness to cooperate. Being part of a team or performance group helps students see the need to sacrifice for the common good.

Intellectual integrity: The practice of self-criticism and the willingness to accept unpalatable facts and the ability to change one's beliefs in the light of changing condition. This includes the capacity for critical judgments and the realization of one's vulnerability to prejudice.

Tolerance: Respect for individuals of different classes, races, religions, customs, and political ideologies. Working toward a common

Table 10.1   Comparison of Key Attributes Developed through Global Education and the Related Arts.

Case's Cognitive and Affective Attributes Developed through Global Education	Bereday and Lauwery's Attributes Developed through the Related Arts
Open-mindedness: being willing to base beliefs on the impartial consideration of available information.	*Unselfishness:* accepting that the common good is of greater value than your immediate interest.
Anticipation of complexity: looking beyond simplistic explanations of complex issues and seeing the interrelationship of factors that created the issue.	*Intellectual integrity:* practicing self-criticism and accepting unpalatable facts in the light of changing conditions.
Resistance to stereotyping: seeing beyond a narrow range of characteristics for individuals from a particular culture or nation.	*Tolerance:* respecting individuals of different classes, races, religions, customs, and political ideologies.
Inclination to emphasize: being willing to place yourself in the role or predicament of another or to imagine issues from another's perspective.	*Justice:* respecting the rights of other people and refusing to claim for yourself a right that you would not concede to others.
Nonchauvinism: avoiding prejudging those with whom you aren't affiliated and to accept the interests of others even if they are incompatible with your own.	*Sensitivity:* being interested in the lives and problems of other people.
	Restraint: accepting of the need to compromise and understanding the evils of tension, hatred, intolerance, prejudice, and war.
	Involvement: wanting to make a personal contribution to the reduction of world problems.

goal within a group that includes those from diverse backgrounds creates an atmosphere where tolerance and respect are developed.

Justice: Respect for the rights of other people and the refusal to claim for oneself a right that one would not grant to others.

Sensitivity: The quality of imagination that leads to an interest in the lives and problems of other people.

Restraint: The acceptance of the need to compromise and an appreciation of the difficult problems of tension, hatred, intolerance, prejudice, and war.

Involvement: A sense of belonging to the human family and the need to make a personal contribution to the reduction of world problems.

Participation in the related arts, therefore, provides a perfect environment for development of the very attributes needed to build a global village. What better arena for practicing collaborative planning, teamwork, cooperation, leadership, consensus building, and working toward a common goal than through organized activities of a related arts class? What better arena to model and practice the values needed for the broader world society? What better arena to produce these favorable attitudes toward global understanding?

A way to incorporate these seven attributes into the physical education classroom is through a study of the Olympics because the athletes participating in the games demonstrate these very attributes. Many resources and projects are available on the Internet for such a study. These resources include materials on the history of the Olympics, information concerning the participating countries, and information about the individual games. Examples of useful websites are the following:

- The International Olympic Committee official website, a valuable source of information for teachers wishing to teach about Olympics
- A WebQuest on the Olympic Games in ancient Greece
- The connection between health and the Olympics found at Edgate Summer Games
- Activities designed to foster the Olympic ideals of fair play, international goodwill, and personal excellence

Using technology as an aid, drama, music, and visual art also integrate smoothly with these seven attributes for developing a global perspective. Websites for a variety of foundations and educational organizations sponsor activities and competitions that enable students to share their creative endeavors with other students around the world as they learn more about and become more sensitive toward global issues.

Every four years, the International Child Art Foundation (ICAF) sponsors the Arts Olympiad to help prepare students for a creative and cooperative future. The Olympiad, an international art competition focused on an annual central theme, begins with local and national exhibitions and concludes with the world's largest international children's celebration. One theme, Children's Visions of the Future, depicts children's dreams for the future during a time when war, pollution, AIDS, poverty, and other complex problems are a very real part of their world. Students can register to participate in ICAF activities at the ICAF website, and visitors can view digital reproductions of the winning students' artwork.

The Multicultural Song Index is part of the Multicultural Pavilion website. The idea for this index grew out of a discussion on the Multicultural Discussion Forum about finding practical, effective ways to initiate discussions about multicultural issues in the classroom. Several people suggested the use of popular music, and others followed by contributing lists of songs that provided the initial content for this resource. Visitors to the site are encouraged to contribute their own song lists that deal with global and human rights issues. Music teachers of students in upper grades will find this an invaluable resource for discussion starters and research topics.

The power of providing classroom activities such as these is that they support the seven attributes identified by Bereday and Lauwerys in a nonthreatening environment. Students can openly discuss issues, share their experiences, and orally examine beliefs without worrying about negative consequences. Such activities provide teachers with opportunities for changing attitudes and perceptions.

UNIVERSAL RIGHTS OF CHILDREN TO PLAY

The United Nations Educational, Scientific, and Cultural Organization (UNESCO) in conjunction with the International Council for Health,

Physical Education, Recreation, Sport, and Dance (2000) has proclaimed that all children have the right to play and participate in physical activities and considers access to quality physical education a fundamental human right. The right of every child to play in a safe environment was captured in the 1959 Declaration of the Rights of the Child proclaimed by the United Nations General Assembly. An excerpt from Principle 7 of this Declaration states,

> The child shall have full opportunity for play and recreation, which should be directed to the same purposes as education; society and the public authorities shall endeavor to promote the enjoyment of this right.

To promote this concept of health, fitness, sports, and play as a universal right and to help students develop a global perspective, students from the United States should participate in joint physical education activities with students from around the world. As students enjoy the identical games and sports that students in other countries enjoy, there is a growing sense of kinship with students around the world. The Internet provides a unique avenue for such participation.

One such activity is International Walk to School Week. On this day, students from around the world walk or bike to school rather than taking the bus or riding in the car. Each October, millions of children, parents, teachers, and community leaders across the globe walk to school to celebrate International Walk to School Day. It serves as an opportunity to focus on the importance of physical activity, safety, air quality, and walkable communities. Walk to School activities often become a catalyst for ongoing efforts to increase safe walking and bicycling throughout the year. The official website of International Walk to School Week provides lesson plan ideas and a place to post pictures after the event.

Project ACES (All Children Exercise Simultaneously) takes place on the first Wednesday in May as part of National Physical Fitness and Sports Month and National Physical Education Week. It has been labeled the world's largest exercise class. Millions of children from all over the world exercise together to promote proper health and fitness habits. The Project ACES website provides information on this annual event.

MULTICULTURAL DIMENSIONS OF THE RELATED ARTS

The inclusion of contributions by artists from around the world is part of the national standards for the four major professional organizations of teachers in related arts. The National Art Education Association has as part of its national standards the following objectives for students:

- *They should be able to develop and present basic analyses of works of art* from structural, historical, and cultural perspectives and from combinations of those perspectives.
- *They should have an informed acquaintance with exemplary works of art from a variety of cultures and historical periods* and a basic understanding of historical development in the arts disciplines, across the arts as a whole, and within cultures.

Content Standard 5 of the National Dance Association requires that students demonstrate and understand dance in various cultures and historical periods. The American Alliance for Theatre and Education requires that students develop cultural awareness by researching, evaluating, and synthesizing cultural and historical information to support artistic choices.

The Music Educators National Conference also advocates the inclusion of cultural awareness as an objective for its students and states in Content Standard 9 that students must have an understanding of music in relation to history and culture. The inclusion of a cultural perspective in the music curriculum is known as ethnomusicology (Society for Ethnomusicology, 2004). Ethnomusicology is defined as the study of music in culture or music as culture.

The inclusion of the study of cultures in the curriculum of related arts courses is a first step toward creating a global perspective. To promote cross-cultural awareness, activities of the related arts classrooms should do the following:

- Describe how various cultures move, play, sing, dance, act, and create art
- Demonstrate how people have similar attributes, ambitions, and emotions regardless of country or culture

- Characterize human camaraderie in the form of both competition and cooperation
- Emphasize the possibilities of collaborative planning and execution
- Indicate ways for personal contribution toward the good of the group

Whether students are participating or learning about activities in physical education, playing or listening to music in music class, creating or learning about art in art class, or producing or learning about a play in drama class, students can also learn about the cultural background of what they are studying. This can be done by creating a subject area unit that focuses on a region or country or by teaching the cultural background of any part of the established curriculum.

The physical structure, materials, and rules of games are unique to cultures, environments, and time periods. Even students in lower grades can understand the cultural relation of games. Games around the world share common characteristics because they typically contain elements that reflect some aspect of reality in life, such as foraging for food, fighting wars against enemies, trading, surviving against the elements of nature, and developing cooperative survival skills. Nickell and Kennedy (1987) classified games into different areas that reflect these fundamental characteristics of culture:

- People and nature
- Competition and cooperation
- War and peace
- Roles
- Traditions
- Worldview

Many games played by students in the United States are also played by children across the world. The American game "Duck Duck Goose" also exists in the Czech Republic, where it is known as "Pesek." A version of "Duck Duck Goose" played in Ghana is known as "Antoakyire." Information for this and other games from around the world can be found at the Games Kids Play website. At a website called Traditional Children's Games from Around the World, many of the more popular playground games are listed with information about similar games from around the globe. Not only is information about the game and how it is played provided, but people from the various countries write about the games and their memories of playing the games as children.

One way in which the unit approach can be accomplished in physical education classes is through a study of soccer and the World Cup. The World Cup presents a perfect opportunity to combine instruction about a particular sport and the countries where the sport is played. While learning the fundamentals of playing soccer, students can also learn about the countries and athletes participating in the World Cup. This also provides a great chance to discuss why soccer is not the national sport of the United States. The World Cup History website provides a tremendous amount of information that can be used in physical education classes.

The unit approach can also be used in the visual arts classroom, such as with the study and creation of masks. The Masks from Around the World website is an online shop featuring tribal masks from Africa, India, the Himalayas, Asia, China, Korea, Java, Bali, New Guinea, Northwestern Coastal America, Mexico, Guatemala, the Caribbean, and Native America. Although this is a commercial site, beautiful photographs of each mask are accompanied by a description of its artistic elements and cultural importance. Based on this information, students can create their own masks for display purposes or for use in a play or skit that includes an explanation of the cultural implications of the masks.

INTERDISCIPLINARY STUDIES SUPPORT

One powerful result of providing a global perspective to the related arts is that it can supplement classroom instruction in the content areas. Coordination between the related arts and the content areas does not easily happen, however, without prior planning and organization. Often, related arts teachers only need to inform those teaching in the content area that they are willing to incorporate the subject area covered into their curriculum. With teachers working together, students' understanding of the culture studied is deepened and expanded.

Physical education teachers can easily incorporate games from many nations studied in social studies classes. Physical educators can discuss the national origins of various games that students play during the course of the year, whether on the playground ("Hopscotch" from Britain) or in physical education ("Follow the Leader" from New Zealand).

Three trade books that provide useful information are *Kids around the World Play! : The Best Fun and Games from Many Lands* by Arlette N. Braman, *The Multicultural Game Book (Grades 1–6)* by Louise Orlandom, and *Multicultural Games* by Lorraine Barbarash. The Internet is another useful source for finding games and sports that relate to a specific country or region. Several countries have either official or unofficial national sports, and in many countries the traditional or official national sports differ from the ones that are currently the most popular.

Locating effective teaching resources for use in related arts classes is often a challenge. One such resource, especially effective for use in interdisciplinary activities, is the Cultural Arts Resources for Teachers and Students (C.A.R.T.S). The C.A.R.T.S. website provides a culture catalog that offers multimedia resources in folklore, history, culture, and the arts for integration across the disciplines. Teachers can also register to join an e-mail list to receive periodic updates about cultural arts resources for teachers and students. Through this site, students can visit with master artists who will share knowledge about their art form, and they can also locate further opportunities to participate in activities for exploring cultures and communities through the arts.

Quilting is one international craft that can be used in an interdisciplinary unit to teach about cultures of diverse ethnic groups. Often, students have grown up sleeping under quilts that tell stories about their own families. Therefore, even primary grade students can comprehend that quilts from around the world also tell stories. Art, history, mathematics, and language arts teachers can work together to present a unit on quilts or quilting. Through a multidisciplinary unit, students can come to understand the aesthetic and historical significance of quilts. Math teachers can use quilts to teach geometric design. Language arts teachers can share family stories through children's books about quilts and quilting.

Lesson plans abound on the Internet for the use of quilts in art, history, language arts, and mathematics classes. At the EDSITEment website, lesson plans on quilts or quilting are designed to help students recognize how people of different cultures and time periods have used cloth-based art forms to pass down their traditions and history. Additional lesson plans are available at the Quiltethnic.com site, which provides links to information about quilts from Africa, Asia, Latin America, and South America.

The enjoyment of quilts can be enhanced though children's books with a quilt theme. Listings of children's books on quilts or quilting are available at the following sites:

- The American Quilting History website, which provides information on some the most notable children's books about quilting
- The Children's Quilting Book website, where more than sixty children's books on quilting can be found
- The Carol Otis Hurst Children's Literature Site, which provides a detailed bibliography of some of the best-known children's books about quilts and quilting
- A Patchwork of Places and Poetry, where a section is devoted to children's books about quilts and quilting

CONCLUSION

Many different techniques, strategies, activities, and routines can be used throughout the curriculum to teach students and influence their perspective toward a more world-conscious and global understanding. When considering all the content knowledge, methods, and techniques of globalizing the curriculum that are included in a typical school day, games, sports, art, music, and drama capture students' enthusiasm and motivation as no other part of the school day can. By capitalizing on students' interests, those things that motivate, excite, and physically involve students provide teachers with a powerful vehicle for global learning, and such involvement cultivates the students' positive global attitudes and universal values.

INSTRUCTIONAL IDEAS

Integrating Physical Education and Web-Based Lessons

"So you want to compete in the Olympics?" is a WebQuest from the online educators' resource Education World. This activity is designed to make students aware of the importance of physical activity and nutrition to maintaining a healthy body, and to provide them with information about the different types of Olympic competitions. The following introduction to this activity for students in grades 3 through 12 sets the stage for the WebQuest. "The International Olympic Committee has decided to hold a Junior Olympics during the next Summer Olympic Games. The committee has invited students from around the world to form teams and participate in that event. You and other students in your class hope to try out for the Junior Olympics, but first you have to plan how you will prepare for the competition."

Students then take on roles such as dietician, trainer, coach, travel agent, treasurer, and statistician. Through their roles they use the websites available through the WebQuest to research to investigate what they need to do to prepare for the Junior Olympics and report on their findings. The task of the activity instructs each team of students to create a PowerPoint presentation explaining what each athlete will need to do to prepare for the Junior Olympics.

To increase global awareness during this activity, teachers might want each team to select a home country to research and include in the final presentation. The WebQuest suggests that each team of students develop a competition involving the sport they chose. Hold a class field day in which students actually participate in those competitions, with each team displaying the flags and colors of their home country.

Integrating Physical Education and Multimedia Presentations

Students can gain a wealth of information about other cultures by researching the history of their games. They can glean much information from the Internet by simply typing "history of games" in a search engine such as Google, resulting in a link to a website such as the Multicultural Games Unit created by students at Germantown Academy in Ft. Washington, Pa., or Online Guide to Traditional Games, from the

United Kingdom. Both of these sites present the cultural history of some common and not-so-common games.

Physical education students might spend some time researching sites like these and create a multimedia project describing the results of their research and instructions for playing the game. A PowerPoint presentation would work well for this project or, if the students have access to digital video cameras, they might create a movie describing the history of the games and demonstrating how the games are played. The presentations can be added to a class website to be shared with others interested in the cultural history of games.

Integrating Related Arts and Telecomputing Projects

Child's Play Touring Theatre (CPTT) from Chicago produces shows for and by students: Writing Our World (WOW!). WOW! presents works that explore children's lives, hopes, and dreams in musical, multicultural performances featuring stories, poems, and songs from villages and towns around the globe. The writings for this show are collected through an online cultural exchange between school students in the United States and in Europe, India, Africa, and other places around the world.

The professional, nonprofit theater is dedicated to performing stories and poems written by young people. In the WOW! project, students are encouraged to explore their own lives and beliefs, as well as those of children in other countries and cultures, with particular emphasis on understanding and celebrating both the differences and the universal commonalities in children throughout the world. The professional actors and directors at Child's Play will read all story submissions and some will be chosen to be performed in the WOW! shows.

Students are invited to submit stories about topics such as their happiest or saddest day, holiday or religious celebrations, stories passed on through families, daily jobs or chores, dreams for the future, descriptions of an "ideal" world, impressions of another country, experiences living in another country, or the most important things in life. Students are encouraged to use their own creativity to come up with great stories and poems, and each time a story is submitted to the website, one of the CPTT sponsors will donate money to help poor families in countries around the world.

Integrating Physical Education and Online Discussions

The goals of the International Council of Sport Science and Physical Education are to contribute to the awareness of human values that are natural in sport and physical activity; to improve health and physical well-being; and to develop physical activity, physical education, and sport in all countries to a high level. In these ways it helps to defend and develop the concept of fair play, the development of the ethical sporting, and the promotion of peace and understanding between people as it attempts to bridge the gap between developed and developing countries.

Located on the ICSSPE website is a link to a forum. This online discussion area allows members of the organization as well as other interested people to share important issues with the sport science and physical education community. The ICSSPE message board is designed to give ICSSPE members and colleagues a voice. Physical education students and their teachers can use this global forum to address topics that the sport science or physical education world needs to consider.

INTERNET RESOURCES

American Quilting History: http://www.womenfolk.com/quilt_books/books_children.htm

Carol Otis Hurst Children's Literature Site: http://www.carolhurst.com/subjects/quilts.html

Children's Quilting Book: http://www.quilt.com/FAQS/BooksChildrenFAQ.html

Child's Play Touring Theatre: http://www.cptt.org/WOW.htm

Cultural Arts Resources for Teachers and Students: http://www.carts.org

Declaration of the Rights of the Child: http://www.unhchr.ch/html/menu3/b/25.htm

Edgate Summer Games: http://www2.edgate.com/summergames/healthy_bodies/

EDSITEment: http://edsitement.neh.gov/view_lesson_plan.asp?id=346

Games Kids Play: http://www.gameskidsplay.net/games/foreign_indexes/index.htm

International Child Art Foundation: http://www.icaf.org/

International Council of Sport Science and Physical Education: http://www.icsspe.org/

International Olympic Committee: http://www.olympic.org/uk/games/index_uk.asp

International Walk to School Week: http://www.iwalktoschool.org/

Masks from Around the World: http://www.masksoftheworld.com

Multicultural Games Unit: http://www.germantownacademy.org/academics/ms/6th/mcgames/Index.htm

Multicultural Pavilion: http://www.edchange.org/multicultural/arts/songs.html

National Sports: http://en.wikipedia.org/wiki/National_sport

Olympic Games in Ancient Greece: http://education.nmsu.edu/webquest/wq/olympics/olympicwq.html

Olympic Ideals: http://www.easynet.net/teamgb/education/

Online Guide to Traditional Games: http://www.tradgames.org.uk/

A Patchwork of Places and Poetry: http://www.mrsmcgowan.com/quilts/books.htm#Quilts

Project ACES—All Children Exercise Simultaneously: http://members.aol.com/acesday/aces.html

Quiltethnic.com: http://www.quiltethnic.com/

So You Want to Compete in the Olympics?: http://www.educationworld.com/a_tech/webquest_orig/webquest_orig008.shtml

Traditional Children's Games from Around the World: http://www.topics-mag.com/edition11/games-section.htm

World Cup History: http://www.worldcup.isn.pl/

REFERENCES

Bereday, G. Z., & Lauwerys, J. A. (1964). *Education and international life.* New York: Harcourt, Brace & World.

Case, R. (1993). Key elements of a global perspective. *Social Education, 57,* 318–323.

International Council for Health, Physical Education, Recreation, Sport, and Dance. (2000, October). A global mission for school physical education. Retrieved October 13, 2004, from http://www.ichpersd.org/i/global.html

Nickell, P., & Kennedy, M. (1987). Global perspectives through children's games. *Social Education, 51,* 1–8.

Society for Ethnomusicology. (2004). Ethnomusicology. Retrieved November 11, 2004, from http://www.indiana.edu/~ethmusic/

Resource Guide

American Forum for Global Education

For more than thirty years, the American Forum has been nationally recognized for providing leadership and assistance to school systems, state departments of education, and colleges and universities. They have initiated hundreds of programs and developed educational materials, teacher training seminars, and publications to guide and implement programs focused on giving young Americans a global perspective as an accepted part of their educational background. The goal of the American Forum is that the young people of the United States will achieve an understanding of global issues, of cultural differences and similarities, and of the connections that exist in their daily lives between their actions—along with those of their country—and those of other groups taking place in all parts of the world. Teachers are provided with teaching materials, lesson plans, professional publications, and study forums.

The American Forum for Global Education
120 Wall St., Suite 2600
New York, NY 10005
212-624-1300 phone
212-624-1412 fax
http://www.globaled.org/

Association for Supervision and Curriculum Development

This group publishes books on global education and sponsors a Global Education Network and its accompanying *Global Connections* newsletter.

Association for Supervision and Curriculum Development
1250 N. Pitt St.
Alexandria, VA 22314
800-933-2733 phone
http://www.ascd.org

Center for Teaching International Relations

The Center for Teaching International Relations (CTIR) prepares youth for increasingly global economic, environmental, and political realities. CTIR is a national leader in developing and publishing educational materials to enhance international understanding in K–12 classrooms. They provide content-rich activities, assessments, and curricula combining creative learning techniques with current academic research. The materials were developed *by* teachers *for* teachers and contain everything needed to bring the world to your classroom.

Center for Teaching International Relations
2201 S. Gaylord St.
Denver, CO 80208
800-967-2847 phone
303-871-2456 fax
http://www.du.edu/ctir/

The Choices Program

CHOICES for the 21st Century is an educational program of the Watson Institute for International Studies at Brown University. Through its curricular resources, professional development workshops, and special projects, CHOICES engages secondary-level students in international issues. Teaching materials and lesson plans are available suitable for high school students.

Choices
Brown University
Providence, RI 02912
401-863-3155 phone
401-863-1247 fax
http://www.choices.edu/index.cfm

Colorado Association of Multicultural Educators

The Colorado Association of Multicultural Educators produces a guide packed with exciting standard-based lessons to integrate multicultural education into the school curriculum. These lessons are in a practical format that may be copied. Most of the lessons are for elementary and middle school students, but some are adaptable to secondary students. To make the lessons easy to use, they include a list of resources, easily prepared materials to supplement the lessons, and even some prepared worksheets and stories.

http://jeffcoweb.jeffco.k12.co.us/passport/lessonplan/lessonindex.ht

Culturegrams

Culturegrams provide teachers with up-to-date information about cultures around the world. The focus is on customs, courtesies, and lifestyles of a culture's people. The children's section provides access to games, maps, flags, recipes, and a chance to hear national anthems.

Culturegrams
800-528- 6279 phone
877-337- 7015 fax
http://www.culturegrams.com

CyberSchoolBus

The United Nations CyberSchoolBus was created in 1996 as the online education component of the Global Teaching and Learning Project, whose mission is to promote education about international issues and the United Nations. The Global Teaching and Learning Project produces high-quality teaching materials and activities designed for educational use (at primary, intermediate, and secondary school levels) and for teacher training. The vision of this project is to provide exceptional educational resources (both online and in print) to students growing up in a world undergoing increased globalization. The specific aims of the CyberSchoolBus are the following:

- To create an online global educational community
- To create educational action projects to show students that they have a role in finding solutions to global problems
- To give students a voice in global issues
- To provide high-quality teaching resources to a wide range of educators in a cost-effective manner

http://www.cyberschoolbus.un.org/

Educators for Social Responsibility

Educators for Social Responsibility helps educators create safe, caring, respectful, and productive learning environments. They help educators work with students to develop the social skills, emotional competencies, and qualities of character that they need to succeed in school and become contributing members of their communities. This group publishes curriculum material on violence prevention and conflict resolution, including conflicts around the world.

Educators for Social Responsibility
23 Garden St.
Cambridge, MA 02138
617-492-1764 phone
617-864-5164 fax
http://www.esrnational.org/

ePALS

More than 4.5 million students and teachers are building skills and enhancing learning with ePALS. Established in 1996, ePALS has 93,510 classroom profiles bringing people in 191 countries together as cross-cultural learning partners and friends. Educators, parents, and students of all ages use ePALS to do the following:

- Safely meet using moderated discussion boards and password-protected chat rooms
- Contribute to international, multilingual, collaborative projects
- Create and use monitored email accounts to help keep inappropriate material from children
- Find partners and friends worldwide quickly and easily with their search tool
- Overcome language barriers with instant translation
- Take advantage of resources offered by ePALS and their carefully chosen partners

ePALS
353 Dalhousie St., 3rd Floor
Ottawa, ON K1N 7G1, Canada
613-562-9847 phone
613-562-4768 fax
http://www.epals.com/

Global Education

This Australian site aims to raise awareness and understanding among school students concerning international issues, development, and poverty and to prepare them to live in an increasingly globalized world and be active citizens shaping better futures. The strategy of the project is to provide an Internet site and curriculum material that is of high professional standard, teacher friendly, and accessible. As well as country profiles and information about global issues, the site contains teaching and learning support materials, teaching ideas and activities, case studies, a professional development event notice board, a monthly newsletter, and links to selected high-quality, relevant AusAID and EdNA Online resources.

Global Education
178 Fullarton Rd.
Dulwich, SA 5065, Australia
61-8-8334-3210 phone
61-8-8334-3211 fax
http://globaleducation.edna.edu.au/

Global Education Center

The Global Education Center, a nonprofit, nongovernmental organization committed to global education, has resource materials (Web resources, print materials, simulation games, and periodicals) for primary and secondary students that teachers can borrow or buy. The website provides links to resources categorized by subject. Perhaps the most useful are Glimpse Kits, which provide glimpses of life in Indonesia, India, the Philippines, Sri Lanka, and Vietnam.

Global Education Center (SA) Inc.
1st Floor, Torrens Building
220 Victoria Square
Adelaide, SA 5000, Australia
08-8221-6744 phone
08-8221-6755 fax
http://www.global-education.asn.au/

Global History Sourcebook

The Global History Sourcebook is dedicated to the exploration of interactions between world cultures. Specifically, this means assessing the ways in which cultures contact each other, the ways they influence each other, and the ways in which new cultural forms emerge.

Fordham University
History Department
Dealy Hall, Room 613
441 E. Fordham Rd.
Bronx, NY 10458

718-817-3925 phone
718-817-4680 fax
http://www.fordham.edu/halsall/global/globalsbook.html

Global Learning Portal

Global Learning Portal (GLP) uses the Internet to help teachers participate in global communities of educators without ever traveling abroad. Through GLP, teachers around the world can share and collaboratively develop education-focused resources such as lesson plans, reports, and case studies. GLP members can create personal profiles so that users are able to find colleagues around the globe who are interested in collaboration. They can explore education-related topics through discussion forums and work together on projects.

Global Learning Portal
1825 Connecticut Ave. NW
Washington, DC 20009
202-884-8000 phone
202-884-8466 fax
http://eportal2-ssdc.aed.org/GLPNetPortal/portal/cn/DefaultContainer
   Page/Site%20Tour

Global SchoolNet

Global SchoolNet's mission is to identify, support, and encourage effective practices and programs that engage students in meaningful content and personal exchanges with people around the world. This allows students to develop basic and advanced literacy and communication skills, creates multicultural understanding, and prepares them for full participation as productive and effective citizens in an increasingly global economy. Global SchoolNet provides the resources to teachers for teaching ideas that bridge geographic gaps through Web publishing, videoconferencing, and other online tools. Global SchoolNet is a growing international network of more than 70,000 online educators who engage in online project-based learning activities. Since its inception, Global SchoolNet has reached more than a million students from 25,000 schools across one hundred countries.

Global SchoolNet
132 N. El Camino Real, Suite 395
Encinitas, CA 92024
760-635-0001 phone
760-635-0003 fax
http://www.globalschoolnet.org

Global TeachNet

Global TeachNet is the premier professional development network for global educators. Its membership includes K–12 teachers, postsecondary educators, and nongovernmental organization representatives. Membership provides the following:

- A bimonthly newsletter, *Global TeachNet*
- A quarterly magazine, *WorldView*
- A weekly listserv announcement of global education opportunities in the United States and abroad
- Annual Homestay Summer Travel Program
- Eligibility for Global Educator Awards ($500) and Peace Educator Awards ($500) (for K–12 school-based educators only)
- An online catalog of award-winning programs with information on successful teacher-developed programs
- Advance notice of GTN and NPCA conferences and workshops

Global TeachNet
1900 L St. NW, Suite 205
Washington, DC 20036
202-293-7728 phone
202-293-7554 fax
http://www.rpcv.org/pages/globalteachnet.cfm

The Globalist

The Globalist Explorer Channel is an online learning tool designed to prepare middle school and high school students around the world to become confident and competent global citizens. The Globalist Explorer Channel advances global and intercultural thinking in the classroom through challenging features with a global perspective. Each week, subscribers receive a dialogue-style fact sheet and a question-and-answer-style quote collection, followed by a quiz and two short essays.

The Globalist
McPherson Square
927 15th St. NW
Washington, DC 20005
202-898-4760 phone
http://www.theglobalist.com/

The GLOBE Program

GLOBE is a worldwide hands-on, primary and secondary school–based education and science program. GLOBE provides the opportunity to learn by doing the following:

- Taking scientifically valid measurements in the fields of atmosphere, hydrology, soils, and land cover/phenology, depending on their local curricula
- Reporting their data through the Internet
- Creating maps and graphs on the free interactive website to analyze data sets
- Collaborating with scientists and other GLOBE students around the world

http://www.globe.gov/fsl/welcome.html

Globetrotter Research Galleries

Drawing from the "Conversations with History" archive of interviews, these research galleries collect the thoughts of a wide range of individuals on specific ideas, events, and histories. The galleries include excerpts from interviews in text or video/audio formats as well as texts from e-mail exchanges, biographical information, and other links on the topic.

Globetrotter Research Galleries
Institute of International Studies
University of California
Berkeley, CA
http://globetrotter.berkeley.edu/PubEd/research/

Intercultural Email Classroom Connections

Intercultural Email Classroom Connections (IECC) is dedicated to helping teachers connect with other teachers to arrange intercultural e-mail connections between their students. IECC is a free teaching.com service to help teachers link with partners in other cultures and countries for e-mail classroom pen-pal e-mail exchanges and other similar projects. Since its creation in 1992, IECC has distributed more than 28,000 requests for e-mail partnerships.

http://www.iecc.org

Intercultural Press

This group publishes curricula, culture guides, and videos on international education.

Intercultural Press
P.O. Box 700
Yarmouth, ME 04096
866-372-2665 phone
207-846-5181 fax
http://www.interculturalpress.com/shop/home.html

International Board on Books for Young People

The International Board on Books for Young People (IBBY) is a nonprofit organization that represents an international network of people from all over the world who are committed to bringing books and children together. IBBY was founded in Zurich, Switzerland, in 1953; today, it is composed of more than sixty-eight national sections all over the world. IBBY publishes *Bookbird: A Journal of International Children's Literature*, which is a refereed journal published quarterly. IBBY also sponsors International Children's Book Day on April 2 of each year to celebrate and inspire a love of reading.

IBBY
Nonnenweg 12, Postfach CH-4003
Basel, Switzerland
4161-272-29-17 phone
4161-272-27-57 fax
http://www.ibby.org/index.html

International Education and Resource Network

The International Education and Resource Network (iEARN) is a nonprofit organization made up of more than 20,000 schools in more than 109 countries. iEARN empowers teachers and young people to work together online using the Internet and other new communications technologies. Approximately 750,000 to 1,000,000 students each day are engaged in collaborative project work worldwide. iEARN has pioneered online school linkages to enable students to engage in meaningful educational projects with peers in their own countries and around the world. These projects are designed to improve the quality of life on the planet. This vision and purpose is what holds iEARN together, enabling participants to become global citizens who make a difference by collaborating with their peers around the world.

International Education and Resource Network
iEARN-USA
475 Riverside Dr., Suite 450

New York, NY 10115
212-870-2693 phone
http://www.iearn.org/

LearnPeace

This website brings together resources that are of interest to students, teachers, and parents. The educational process and its content are not value free, and neither is the material available here. The value that underpins this site is the belief that nonviolence is better than violence, that building a culture of peace should be a priority, and a part of this process is both to question and to challenge the complacency in a culture of violence.

LearnPeace
1 Peace Passage
London N70BT, United Kingdom
44-020-7424-9444 phone
44-020-7482-6390 fax
http://www.ppu.org.uk/indexa.html

Multicultural Pavilion

Multicultural Pavilion provides resources for educators, students, and activists to explore and discuss multicultural education; to facilitate opportunities for educators to work toward self-awareness and development; and to provide forums for educators to interact and collaborate toward a critical, transformative approach to multicultural education. Links include the following:

- Teacher's corner
- Education resource room
- Awareness activities
- Quips and quotations
- Listserv
- Multicultural awareness quiz
- Poetry e-journal

- Multicultural song index
- Film reviews

http://www.edchange.org/multicultural/

National Geographic Educational Series

This site provides books, curricular materials, and online projects. National Geographic Kids Network provides online activities for students. The National Geographic Education link provides lesson plans, photos, and activities for classroom use.

National Geographic Education Services
1145 17th St. NW
Washington, DC 20036-4688
800-647-5463 phone
http://www.nationalgeographic.com/education/

Peace Education Foundation

The mission of the Peace Education Foundation is to educate children and adults in the dynamics of conflict and to promote skills in peacemaking in homes, schools, communities, nations, and the world. This site offers curricular materials on conflict resolution, mediation, and decision making.

Peace Education Foundation
1900 Biscayne Blvd.
Miami, FL 33131
800-749-8838 phone
305-576-3106 fax
http://www.peaceeducation.com/

Skipping Stones Magazine

Skipping Stones is a nonprofit children's magazine that encourages co-operation, creativity, and celebration of cultural and environmental richness. It provides a playful forum for sharing ideas and experiences among children from different lands and backgrounds. *Skipping Stones* contains stories, articles, and photos from all over the world. Non-English writings are accompanied by English translations to encourage the learning of various languages. Each issue also contains international pen pals, book reviews, news, and a guide for parents and teachers. The guide offers creative activities and resources for making the best use of *Skipping Stones* in your home or classroom. Many articles are available online.

Skipping Stones Magazine
P.O. Box 3939
Eugene, OR 97403
541-342-4956 phone
http://www.skippingstones.org/index.html

Teacher Talk Forum

The Center for Adolescent and Family Studies (CAFS) is a research center in the School of Education at Indiana University. It sponsors the Teacher Talk Forum, which is a resource for practitioners, teachers, and families that provides information through this website, including professional papers, presentations, and other print media. Information provided includes Internet Field Trips, Technology in the Classroom, Lesson Plans, Cyber Schools, Museums, and References for Kids.

Teacher Talk Forum
Eigenmann Hall, 5th Floor, Room 509
1900 E. 10th St.
Bloomington, IN 47408
812-855-2355 phone
812-855-1847 fax
http://www.iub.edu/%7Ecafs/ttforum/ttforum.html

Teaching for Change

Teaching for Change is a not-for-profit organization based in Washington, D.C. It is a resource of videos, children's books, and materials for teachers on diverse cultures and countries as well as issues of inequity, prejudice, and conflict.

Teaching for Change
P.O. Box 73038
Washington, DC 20056
800-763-9131 phone
http://www.teachingforchange.org/

Teaching Tolerance

Teaching Tolerance supports the efforts of K–12 teachers and other educators to promote respect for differences and an appreciation of diversity. Teaching Tolerance serves as a clearinghouse of information about antibias programs and activities being implemented in schools across the country. Teaching Tolerance also produces and distributes free, high-quality antibias materials. They develop resources that speak to various academic subject areas and grade levels because tolerance education is the responsibility of every teacher.

Teaching Tolerance
A Project of the Southern Poverty Law Center
400 Washington Ave.
Montgomery, AL 36104
334-956-8374 phone
http://www.tolerance.org/teach

U.S. Department of State and U.S. Department of Education

Each November, the U.S. Department of State and the U.S. Department of Education sponsor International Education Week. This week is an opportunity to celebrate the benefits of international education and exchange worldwide. The website provides downloadable materials that include brochures and a variety of curricular activities.

International Education Week
Office of Global Educational Programs (ECA/A/S/A)

Bureau of Educational and Cultural Affairs
U.S. Department of State Annex 44
301 4th St. SW, Room 349
Washington, DC 20547
202-205-2452 fax
http://exchanges.state.gov/iew

World Peace Project for Children

The mission of the World Peace Project for Children is to promote world peace by educating children about global matters that concern them and by giving them tools to build positive connections with children in other cultures. Available here is a Peace Education Kit.

World Peace Project for Children
P.O. Box 1253
Issaquah, WA 98027
425-391-3745 phone
425-391-4797 fax
http://www.sadako.org/

World Wise Schools

Coverdell World Wise Schools (CWWS) is an innovative education program that seeks to engage learners in an inquiry about the world, themselves, and others. Initially set up as a correspondence "match" program between volunteers and U.S. classes, World Wise Schools has expanded its scope over the past ten years by providing a broad range of resources for educators—including award-winning videos, teacher guides, classroom speakers, a newsletter, and online resources.

Peace Corps
World Wise Schools
1111 20th St. NW
Washington, DC 20526

800-424-8580 ext. 1450 phone
202-692-1450 phone
202-692-1421 fax
http://www.peacecorps.gov/wws

Index

About the Authors

Anne Wall, assistant professor of education at Austin Peay State University in Clarksville, Tennessee, completed her doctoral degree in education at Tennessee State University. She earned a master's degree in curriculum and instruction with a specialization in instructional technology from Austin Peay and a bachelor's degree from the University of Kansas. She taught fifth grade in the Clarksville-Montgomery County School System, where she was named teacher of the year for Burt School and received the WSMV Apple for the Teacher Award. In 2000, she was awarded the International Reading Association's Presidential Award for Reading and Technology for the Southeast region. She has served as secretary of the Tennessee Reading Association and vice president of the Mid-Cumberland Reading Council. She is a member of the International Reading Association, the Association for the Advancement of Computing in Education, and the International Society for Technology in Education.

Since 2001, Dr. Wall has presented widely at regional, national, and international conferences. She recently published an article with Dr. Carlette Hardin and Dr. Ann Harris, "Visual Verse: Using Images to Enhance Poetry Instruction," in *Changing Tides 2004 Selected Readings*, the journal of the International Visual Literacy Association.

Carlette Hardin is professor of education at Austin Peay State University, Clarksville, Tennessee. Dr. Hardin has degrees from Austin Peay State University (B.S. and M.S.) and Vanderbilt (Ed.D.). Dr. Hardin has been active in professional organizations at the state and national levels, having served as president of the National Association for Developmental Education. Dr. Hardin has given over 100 keynote addresses, presentations, and workshops at state, regional, and national conferences.

Since 1981, Dr. Hardin has had numerous professional publications and funded grants. Her article "Access to Higher Education: Who Belongs?" was the outstanding article for the 1988–1989 volume of the *Journal of Developmental Education*. A ten-year review was recently published in a chapter of *Developmental Education and Its Role in Preparing College Students* by the University of South Carolina Press. Dr. Hardin and Dr. Ann Harris have written a fastback, *Managing Classroom Crises*, for Phi Delta Kappa, published in the spring of 2000. An orientation textbook for adult students, *100 Things Every Adult Student Ought to Know*, was published in February 2000 by Cambridge University Press. Dr. Hardin authored *Effective Classroom Management: Models and Strategies for Today's Classroom*, published by Merrill/Prentice Hall in 2004.

Ann Harris is a professor of education at Austin Peay State University. She has taught in the public schools prior to receiving her doctoral degree and master's degree from Memphis State University. She is a reading specialist and teaches methods classes at the undergraduate and graduate levels. At the national and international levels, she is a member of the International Reading Association, the National Council of Teachers of English, the National Middle School Association, the International Visual Literacy Association, and Phi Delta Kappa. She is currently serving as the International Reading Association state coordinator for Tennessee. She served six years as editor of the state newsletter for the Tennessee Reading Association. She has served as chairperson on numerous committees and in various officer positions at the international, state, and local levels. She has conducted numerous presentations at these professional associations at national, state, and local levels. She is very active in the local public schools, serving as a consultant on Balanced Literacy, serving as facilitator for School Improvement Projects, and conducting professional development sessions on various aspects of literacy.

Her recent publications include a Phi Delta Kappan fastback with Dr. Carlette Hardin titled *Managing Classroom Crises* and a chapter titled "Historical Trends in Bibliotherapy: Books That Help Children Cope" in G. M. Duhon and T. J. Manson (eds.), *Preparation, Collaboration, and Emphasis on the Family in School Counseling for the New Millennium*. She has written many journal articles and funded grants and has been awarded the prestigious Outstanding Educator Award by Phi Delta Kappa and the Distinguished Professor Award by the Tennessee Reading Association.